"Everyone longs for an intimate marriage. And Jim Burns, after more than three decades of marriage with Cathy, shows us how we can have just that. This is a book with heart. Don't miss out on its message."
—**Drs. Les & Leslie Parrott,** Seattle Pacific University, authors of *Love Talk*

"Marriages are 'made,' not 'born' at the wedding altar. Marriages can be intimate and supportive, or distant and destructive. . . . Jim Burns offers practical ideas for those who want to create an intimate and supportive marriage."
—**Gary D. Chapman, PhD,** Author of *The Five Love Languages*

"In *Creating an Intimate Marriage,* Jim Burns is not only a trusted counselor but a transparent one as well. Whether your marital fire is slowly fading or has long been extinguished, married couples will appreciate his wisdom and personal experience in rekindling the spark we all long for with our spouse."
—**Hayley DiMarco,** Author of *Dateable* and *Marriable*

"As a student in Jim's youth ministry many years ago, I began to watch his marriage to Cathy. I am honored to have had a front-row seat, which is why I can confidently recommend this book to you. Jim's heart is for your marriage not only to be healthy and God honoring, but that your family would be blessed by the legacy an intimate marriage will create. This book will touch your heart and challenge you to desire God's best for your marriage."
—**Doug Fields,** Purpose Driven Youth Ministry, Saddleback Church

"Here's an inspiring and practical guidebook to marriage as God intended. Thanks, Jim, for this indispensable new resource!"
—**Lee Strobel,** Author of *The Case for Christ* and *The Case for a Creator*

"Jim has given us a gift in this book. He provides a very practical path to helping a struggling relationship, or to making a good one better. Very sound, usable advice."
—**Dr. Henry Cloud,** Author of *Boundaries, Integrity: The Courage to Meet the Demands of Reality*

"No one wants a marriage that looks and feels like a business partnership. There is a deep need for intimacy and connection in relationships. Jim Burns does a wonderful job of providing the blueprint for physical, emotional, and relational intimacy. This is life-changing and marriage-enriching material."

—**Dr. Kevin Leman,** Author of *Sheet Music: Uncovering the Secrets of Sexual Intimacy in Marriage*

"Creating an intimate marriage isn't just *knowing* what to do but *doing* what you know. Rarely do we see a book that does both! In a very practical, encouraging way Jim Burns will challenge you to make your marriage a priority and give you the steps to actually do it. This book should be required reading for all marriages at any stage of life. We highly recommend it!"

—**David & Claudia Arp,** Authors of the 10 GREAT DATES series and *Suddenly They're 13: Or the Art of Hugging a Cactus*

"If you want to experience more intimacy and fulfillment in your marriage, apply Jim's principles! This book will speak volumes of wisdom, revelation, and encouragement to both husbands and wives, providing a clear road map to having an A.W.E.some relationship!"

—**Shannon Ethridge, MA,** Bestselling author of the *Every Woman's Battle* series

"Whether your marriage is shaky or on solid ground, Jim Burns' book will help you discover real intimacy through practical, fun, biblical principles that will enrich your marriage and deepen your love for each other."

—**Bo Boshers,** Executive Director, Student Ministries, Willow Creek Association

"I am in *awe* of Jim Burns' ability to provide conviction and hope at the same time. *Creating an Intimate Marriage* is one of the few books on marriage with the courage to tackle real problems and provide practical solutions."

—**Ray Johnston,** President, Developing Effective Leaders; Senior Pastor, Bayside Church, Granite Bay, California

Creating an Intimate Marriage

Rekindle Romance Through
Affection, Warmth, & Encouragement

JIM BURNS

BETHANY HOUSE PUBLISHERS

Minneapolis, Minnesota

Creating an Intimate Marriage
Copyright © 2006
Jim Burns

Cover design by Lookout Design, Inc.

Published by Bethany House Publishers
11400 Hampshire Avenue South
Bloomington, Minnesota 55438

Bethany House Publishers is a division of
Baker Publishing Group, Grand Rapids, Michigan.

Printed in the United States of America

ISBN   978-0-7642-0405-0

To Cathy

Wife, Partner, Friend, Hero

Books by Jim Burns

FROM BETHANY HOUSE PUBLISHERS

Accept Nothing Less
Closer
Confident Parenting
Confident Parenting DVD Kit
Creating an Intimate Marriage
Creating an Intimate Marriage Audiobook
Creating an Intimate Marriage DVD Kit
God Made Your Body
How God Makes Babies
The Purity Code
The Purity Code Audio Resource
Teaching Your Children Healthy Sexuality
Teaching Your Children Healthy Sexuality DVD Kit
Teaching Your Children Healthy Sexuality Parent/Child Combo Pack
Teenology

Acknowledgments

Thank you . . .

Cindy Ward . . . for your incredible help and assistance. You set a most positive tone and atmosphere in our office. Your light shines brightly.

Todd Dean . . . for your leadership and giftedness at HomeWord. You and God have orchestrated a miracle. I will be forever grateful.

Randy Bramel, Tom Purcell, Bucky Oltmans, and Terry Hartshorn . . . for your inspiration every Tuesday morning. I am so honored to be in your group.

Jon Wallace . . . for your friendship and role model of a leader. I look forward to every time we hang out.

Helen and Lee Lovaas . . . for believing in the HomeWord mission. Your quiet generosity has made a bigger difference than you may ever understand this side of heaven.

Kyle Duncan . . . for your belief in me. Together we will change the world.

Jeanne Hedrick . . . for not only a wonderful job of editing this manuscript, but for being a joy to work with on this project.

Greg Johnson . . . for exceptionally great work as a literary agent. I'm proud to have you represent me.

Christy, Rebecca, and Heidi Burns . . . for being my inspiration. I am a father most blessed. I would have written this book to help your marriages even if no one else read it!

Contents

Foreword

Most everyone who marries has high hopes and expectations of an intimate marriage. While dating we try to eliminate the other potentials who just don't seem to have all that we want and need in a spouse. And then, somehow we stumble onto someone that starts the adrenaline pumping, the eyes sparkling, and the dreams developing. High hopes and low maintenance keep the relationship humming along toward Holy Matrimony. You find yourself so in love that just hearing the other person breathe so melts you that it is obvious you are in the presence of a soul mate. Hours and hours of talking prove that this is the real thing as poetic and profound words stream forth from your mouths. Shakespeare would not have the words to describe these feelings of romance, and there is nothing left to do but make plans and start shopping for rings.

Scientists have studied this phase of a relationship, and they are not so enchanted. Some researchers equate this phase of romance and infatuation to mental illness, obsessive-compulsive disorder, or addiction. I have conducted my own study and have come to believe that there is within the wedding cake a secret ingredient that all bakers covertly add to the mix. Once the wedding cake is eaten, everything seems to change for most people.

The dream of an intimate marriage is replaced with "infinite" times. The infinities are different for each partner. For one partner, the ears wilt listening to talks that go on and on for what seems like an infinity, while the other partner feels like it is infinity before the other even grunts or shows some sign of acknowledgment that there is a person trying to communicate. For one it seems like an infinity between sexual encounters, and for the other an infinity before the other is satisfied. One takes an infinite amount of time in the bathroom, and the other spends an infinite amount of time watching television while grasping a remote control like it is a sacred object used in the practice of a solitary religion, which it actually is. Infinity replaces intimacy in so many marriages that it would seem like an infinity to count them all.

Shortly after the icing has been wiped from each other's lips it starts to feel like the other partner just does not get it when it comes to meeting needs. Weren't they listening during those days of courtship? And where did all these demands from the other side come from? What was low maintenance now needs more attention than a Yugo. The Prince came with a horse and the daily task seems to be to clean up after the beast, whichever one fits that classification. The Princess came with nails and they must be allowed to dry and remain undamaged for a fortnight. Your soul mate seems more like a cold mate and you find yourself in a stalemate.

Holy Matrimony is now filled with phrases like Holy Moses and Holy Toledo and Holy Moley because the partnership causes some very unholy reactions. Even your partner's breathing is so irritating that private bedrooms may be an option if a cork does not work. Rather than words more beautiful than Shakespeare, all you want to do is shake your partner, and a spear seems like a handy tool to have lying around the house. For months it felt like you were on drugs and now you may resort to them if things don't pick up soon. The only people you are more disappointed in than your spouse are all of the married couples who knew this was going to happen but refused to let you in on their little secret, because misery loves company.

So it is with so many who wanted so much from a marriage. If my exaggerated account rings a bit true in your relationship, you have come to the right place or at least the right book. Jim Burns has put together some concepts from his own marriage (a marriage I have admired through the years), his education (Princeton did a really good job or at least he did a really good job at Princeton), working with families (a friend used to claim to have counseled half of Orange County, but Jim actually has), books he has read (he was stopped at airport security once because of all the sex books in his carryon he was taking to Hawaii to read in preparation for a talk), and some great interviews (his radio show puts him in front of the best minds and the deepest thinkers of our day. I don't think he has had the Pope on, but since he has never been married he wouldn't have helped Jim on this book). I don't think you are going to be disappointed in what you read and learn here.

I have to admit I have a bad attitude about marriage books. Most of them are not very interesting, and many of them are just plain wrong. Some will tell you that if you take care of all the elements of a loving relationship, the intimacy will take care of itself. That just is not true. Take care of developing the intimacy and you will partner to address and work together on all of the other elements of the relationship. Jim has done a great job here, teaching us how to connect without it being a chore and how to create intimate moments that both spouses can enjoy. His insights on the fast pace we lead are right on target. Our pace destroys our passion and eliminates time for it. But it is not just about slowing the pace; it is about two people operating at the same pace with romantic intentionality. Two people wanting a better marriage and willing to do whatever it takes to achieve it will find intimacy.

If you are like me, you often approach nonfiction books with a stubborn arrogance that does not believe there is anything new to learn; you figure you pretty much know it all. I hope it does not take a marriage falling apart before you realize, like I did, that there is a lot to learn. All of us need to replace our stubborn arrogance with humble willingness. If you will do that as you approach this great book by Jim Burns, I believe you will unlock some of the secrets that will lead you to cooperation, teamwork, connection, and a divine intimacy that too few ever discover. But it can be yours, if you are willing. I hope you find what you are looking for, not in this book, but in the eyes of your spouse. And I hope your spouse finds in you a humble and open heart that builds intimacy, romance, and an infinite amount of love.

—Stephen Arterburn

Introduction

You have in your hands a very personal and important book for me. It is not totally biographical, but in many ways it is the journey Cathy and I have been on for more than thirty-one years. We know we still have a lot to learn, but we want to share with you what we have gleaned so far. I probably had the head knowledge and research information to write this book several years ago, but I didn't have the years of maturity and experience needed to share what I believe are some of the most important principles in creating a more intimate marriage. There is no doubt in my mind that this book will disturb you, inspire you, give you some great ideas, and also help you realize (as if you didn't already know this) that to bring more connection, intimacy, and spirituality to your marriage will take a great deal of focus.

If you are anything like me, you probably have a "high-maintenance" marriage. This means you possibly walked down the aisle with your spouse with the notion that marriage would be easier for you than for others. By now you have probably figured out that marriage is wonderful . . . but not easy. Too many marriages are over-committed and under-connected. There are so many competing priorities that confuse our relationship, including the attention we give to our kids instead of our spouse. There are days when Cathy and I have been "dangerously tired" because of our hectic schedule with kids, work, church, and all our outside activities. The result? We just didn't have the energy to focus on each other. There have been seasons of marriage when it seemed conducive to connection, and other seasons when it felt more like a business relationship than an intimate marriage.

You and I didn't sign up for marriage to make it turn out more like a business partnership than an intimate connection of love, respect, romance, and spiritual oneness. Far too many couples settle for mediocrity in their marriage when they would never settle for second-best in other areas of their life. I want to encourage you to set a tone of affection, warmth, and encouragement in your relationship that will result in rekindling the romance in your marriage. Will it take some work? You bet it will! Will it be worth it? Absolutely.

My hope and prayer is that the words in this book will bring as much healing and health to your relationship as they have to mine. If there is anything we can do at HomeWord to come alongside your marriage and your parenting, do not hesitate to contact us at *www.HomeWord.com*. Our daily radio program, broadcast all across America and on the Internet, is also a great resource for you. I hope we not only develop a relationship through this book but also continue that relationship through the many avenues of service we provide at HomeWord.

One of the phrases that I have to remember as a speaker and writer is that "people learn best when *they* communicate, not when *I* communicate." With this thought in mind, I have created a section at the end of every chapter that will help you ask and answer questions that will cause you to go deeper in your relationship with your spouse and within your own life as well. I really encourage you to take the time to read the chapters together and then answer the questions. There is a set of questions for you alone to answer (*Questions for Me*), and one for you and your spouse to answer together (*Questions for Us*). A final set of questions are to help you put into practice some of the principles taught within that chapter. These questions are called *Heart-to-Heart HomeWork*. (Don't let the word *homework* scare you! You'll love the practical applications in this section.) Most often, the best transformation in a marriage comes from genuine, honest, loving conversation with your spouse, so take the time and effort needed to complete this part of the book.

If you find this book helpful, you may also want to create a small group with the help of our "Creating an Intimate Marriage Transformation Kit." HomeWord has developed a program for small groups of couples who desire to have a more intimate marriage to meet together and work through some of the material in conjunction with this book. It includes DVDs of my speaking, participant guides, etc. More information on this kit can be found at the back of this book on the HomeWord ministry pages.

Again, I am honored you would take the time to read this book and invest in your marriage. Your courage to make a difference in your relationship may be the most important investment you make in the legacy of your life and family.

Jim Burns
Dana Point, California

Making Your Marriage
Your Top Priority

Cathy and I have been married for more than thirty-one years. I truly am a fortunate person. God knew what He was doing and I didn't. We describe our relationship as a "high-maintenance marriage." This means we have to constantly work at keeping our relationship healthy. Marriage doesn't come easy for us. We have felt at times like hypocrites speaking and writing on the subject. At other times we've wondered if our message and strategy for an intimate marriage would work for anyone else like it has for us. To be perfectly honest, I never set out to write a book on marriage or to speak on the subject.

Several years ago my good friends at Youth Specialties asked me to do an eight-hour "Ministry and Marriage" session for church leaders and their spouses at a national convention. At first I turned them down. I told them I had never spoken on the subject for more than twenty minutes, let alone eight hours. I was definitely not an expert. They had access to any marriage expert in the country to give the seminar, so I encouraged them to find someone else to do it.

They came back and said, "We still want you." And in a weak moment I said yes. Basically, that first eight-hour session was filled with information about issues that Cathy and I struggled with in our marriage and offered some very simple and practical ideas for refreshing their marriages. It wasn't the most articulate seminar ever given and, frankly, it wasn't all that well researched either. I was the most surprised person on the planet at the incredibly positive response. I was struck with two thoughts after the first conference: (1) Cathy and I weren't the only ones who had a high-maintenance marriage; and (2) people were struggling with figuring out a practical strategy to make their marriage work.

Since that initial conference in the late '80s, Cathy and I have shared these principles with a lot of people. The result is always the same. Couples who truly want to improve their marriage get excited about the possibility for change. They are willing to make courageous decisions to develop a marriage that is far from perfect (Perfect marriages don't exist!), but one that is filled with more intimacy than they have been experiencing.

I wish I could offer you a simple method that would magically change your relationship for the better. I can't. I can only say that *if you are willing to make your marriage a top priority and implement some of the principles in this book, then you will have a very fulfilling marriage.* There will be an additional bonus as well: The improvements to your marriage will also make your children more secure. In fact, I have the audacity to say (humbly, of course!) that unless your marriage is suffering extreme trauma, such as adultery, abuse, addictions, or other major issues, these principles, when applied, can *dramatically and immediately* change your relationship for the better. (In the case of extreme trauma, I urge you to seek a qualified marriage counselor who can help you get to a point where this book will be helpful.)

THE TURNING POINT

Cathy and I came to a major turning point in our marriage at the Salt and Pepper Diner in Orange County, California. The twenty-four-hour restaurant was a "breakfast served all day," wipe your own table down, greasy spoon kind of place. It had become sort of a hangout for Cathy and me, where we could unwind late at night after our Wednesday night youth group meeting. I guess we chose it because it was cheap and right around the corner from our apartment.

Four years earlier, Cathy had graduated from college. One week after that she walked down the aisle to marry me. After a wonderful ten-day honeymoon, I started a new job as a youth worker at a great church in Orange County. Some people have an easy time of it the first years of marriage. We didn't. I can still remember arguing all the way to the church youth group where I was going to speak to the students on "The Beauty of a Christian Home." The whole time I was speaking to them I was wondering if I had made the biggest mistake of my life! I'm sure Cathy was thinking the same thing.

We made it through that very humbling first year of our marriage and moved to Princeton, New Jersey, for my graduate school degree. We continued to work on our marriage with some days of success and other days of questioning our sanity. After graduate school, we came back to California, where I worked at a church as a youth pastor and Cathy taught preschool. Everything looked great on the outside. But inside we both still struggled with our relationship.

Our youth group took off and grew from four kids to over one hundred in just a few months. The kids liked us. The parents liked us. The church loved us and even doubled our salary after the first year. (Some people who work in churches would put doubling a church salary in one year on the same level as a miracle—such as Moses parting the Red Sea! Don't be too impressed, though; it was still a very small salary.) Cathy and I were very busy with the success of the youth group, her job, and our relationships with friends and family.

Being the insensitive male, I didn't even realize that we were investing very little energy into our own marriage relationship.

She was my best youth group volunteer, I was enjoying my job, we had a lot of fun with friends, and we regularly had sex. *Wasn't that all there was to marriage?* My idea of a date was going to a high school football game together, where I would spend most of my time talking with students from the youth group and leave Cathy alone to watch the game by herself.

Back to the Salt and Pepper Diner. After a particularly good youth group meeting one Wednesday night, Cathy and I were sitting at the diner. After we ordered, Cathy looked at me with THAT look. Her lip began to tremble, and I knew this was not going to be a comfortable meal. The lip-tremble thing still gets me, and now my three daughters have the same lip tremble. I think it is hereditary! Anyway, Cathy suddenly blurted out, "I don't know if I want to have children."

I just stared at her in disbelief. This came out of left field and was totally unexpected. It was what kids today call "random." I managed to croak out, "What are you talking about, Cathy?"

"I just don't know if I want to have kids."

"Cathy, we talked about kids on our first date! You teach children—your degrees are in early childhood education! You are the finest person I have ever seen with children! What do you mean, you don't want kids?"

"It's just that our lives are so busy, and you and I have strayed so far apart." She went on to say, "I have been resenting you and the constant negative drain from your work for some time, but now I am even resenting God. Why would our relationship be suffering so much, even with all the good things that are happening with your work?" She continued, "Don't get me wrong. I also see God's hand on our ministry. Even tonight I was so aware of all the kids who are being helped and reached. Nevertheless, all this busyness and lack of focus with our marriage is causing me to question if we should even have kids of our own. They would never see you, and the strain of your work is straining our marriage."

I mentioned a few paragraphs above that this conversation would be a turning point for our marriage. She might as well have socked me in the stomach and taken all the wind out of me. And to make matters worse, I knew she was correct. I didn't have the answers, and frankly, we had very few role models to help us figure out what was the right thing to do.

In response, I just blurted out these words: *"Cathy, I am having an affair."* I quickly qualified it to say it wasn't an affair with another woman. (Or a man, for that matter!) My affair was with my job. My mistress was the church youth group that was taking all my energy and attention. My love affair with my job was causing me to give Cathy only my emotional scraps. My needs, coming out of a low self-image, were being met by my job. I was running toward it, causing a strain in my relationship with Cathy.

My love affair with my job was causing me to give Cathy only my emotional scraps.

RESETTING OUR PRIORITIES

That night, sitting in a booth at the diner, we came up with three priorities. They were simple, but powerful. Truly, I would not be able to write this book if it weren't for the three action steps I wrote on a paper napkin—priorities we began to put into practice right away. Here they are:

1. *A nonnegotiable date night each week*
2. *Away from home only three nights a week*
3. *Cathy to have veto power over my schedule*

Sitting across from each other that night we made a commitment to go out on a *date every week*. It didn't have to be somewhere expensive. When little children came along, we had to trade some baby-sitting with others in the same situation to keep the costs down. Sometimes the date was a cup of coffee and a walk at the harbor near where we live.

During the date, we tried not to talk business. We made it a point (and still do) to focus on each other. It is a time to renew our love and court each other. That means we can't come to the date emotionally spent on everyone else's problems so that we have nothing to give each other. Sure, we miss a date or two in a year, but it is very, very rare. I find that the average couple has a desire to have special dates, but they just don't make it a priority. For those that do, I have never heard any of them say that a regular date together is not a very positive addition to their relationship.

We also decided that we couldn't maintain a healthy marriage relationship if we were gone from our house too many nights. In a recent survey, I read that the average minister in America is out an average of five nights a week. I was out at least that many nights before we made this commitment. Cathy and I decided that *three nights away from home a week* would be our priority. Even if it meant I needed to quit my job, we would stick to our plan of only three nights out a week.

Our relationship changed almost immediately because we spent more time together and didn't live at such a frantic pace. There is nothing magical about three nights as opposed to two or four. It was just that, in our case, we felt this would work best for our high-maintenance marriage. We were amazed to find that we actually could accomplish most of what we had done before.

Far too many couples take on more responsibilities than their marriage can handle. They forget that marriages and family life need time around the dinner table. The reason God made day (light) and night (darkness) was to remind us that we don't have to work ourselves into the ground. Too many activities away from the home will damage family relationships.

The *veto power* decision was a major decision for us. Some of our biggest arguments had happened because of my runaway schedule. That night in the diner, almost like an alcoholic who finally admits that he has no control over his addiction, I said, "Cathy, you can have veto power over our schedule." This didn't mean that she was put in a position of being the bad cop all the time. It simply meant I would bring night, weekend, and travel schedule issues to her *before* making a decision.

By giving her veto power, I began to include her in my life in a new way. Today, we may lament together about our busy schedule or a decision that we made about our calendar, but we don't argue or blame each other anymore because we both had a say in what we're doing. That night, our marriage changed for the better because we did radical surgery on our relationship. But even more than that, I now understand that those decisions brought emotional security to Cathy.

FIRST THINGS FIRST

These may not seem like turning-point resolutions for you, but these three decisions helped us realize that we had to make our marriage a top priority. We had been living with too many "attractive distractions" and "confused priorities." My confused priority was that I often put my work/vocation before my relationship with Cathy.

It is so easy in today's world to develop well-meaning but confused priorities. Some people put money, exercise, football, the kids, the in-laws, shopping, and almost anything else in front of their marriage relationship. Nowhere in the Bible are we called to have "child-focused" marriages. Yet the moment children start coming into the picture, many marriages dissolve into a child-focused relationship. Obviously, we should never neglect our children, but as we look at what honors God, the following is what makes the most sense scripturally:

* *God first*

* *Marriage second*

* *Children and family third*

* *Vocation and other issues next*

When people put *God first* in their lives, they tend to have their other priorities in the right order as well. Jesus said it best in His Sermon on the Mount: "Seek first the kingdom of God and His righteousness, and all these things shall be added to you" (Matthew 6:33 NKJV). As we attempt to place God on the throne of our life, He will help us keep our priorities straight.

As I mentioned, one of the big struggles with marriages today is the tendency to put our kids' needs before those of our spouse. What we don't realize is that child-centered marriages are often weak marriages, and in the long run they hurt the kids more than help them. If your spouse is not getting his or her emotional needs met by you, often he or she will pour all their energy into the children. The end result is an unhealthy marriage relationship.

Obviously, I am not talking about neglecting your children. I just want to emphasize the importance of seeking to keep your marriage vows a major priority. When children see a marriage relationship of integrity, they will feel more secure. In fact, Scripture says, "He who walks with integrity walks securely" (Proverbs 10:9 NKJV).

I am convinced that a marriage of priority and integrity will be one of the best offerings you can provide for your children. You may still need to give extra time and attention to the needs of your kids, especially at certain seasons of their development. However, your kids must also see their mom and dad taking time for each other through regular date nights, daily connection times, appropriate expressions of romance, and even a commitment to time away for replenishing your relationship. I'm sure you have heard the very true statement: "Do your kids a favor and love your spouse."

Do your kids a favor and love your spouse.

The key is not to prioritize what's on your schedule, but to schedule your priorities. You could probably easily describe where your priorities *should* be in your relationship. Acting upon them is another thing. It's not easy. Life, especially married life, is messy. There is no perfect life or marriage this side of heaven. However, our lives will be much better off when we are proactive with our priorities. If you really want to understand priorities, all you have to do is look at children or talk with the elderly. If you ask older people or children what they value, it's always the same things: relationship with God . . . a loving marriage . . . treasured friendships. Basically, it is about a right relationship with God and loved ones.

My Aunt Ann died while I was writing this book. She was one of the great inspirations in my life. I sat with her recently as she talked about her fifty-plus years of marriage to Uncle John, her strong faith, and her extended family. She told stories about her husband who had already passed into eternity, her children, grandchildren, and her beloved garden. As she prepared for her transition from this world to her eternal reward with God, she didn't talk about her financial investments or what grades she received at USC in the '40s. She knew her priorities. Her funeral was a glorious celebration of a life well lived with an eternal perspective. But you don't want to wait until you are older to make your marriage a priority. Now is the time.

CHALLENGES TO OVERCOME

When it comes to marriage, the institution is in trouble. I call it the lonely wife/lonely husband syndrome. They are busy at work, busy with the kids, even busy with their church. Some of these fine couples are weary from well-doing, but one day they look up and realize that they have little relationship with each other. They don't have the energy to invest in their marriage. So they keep on keeping on, living lonely, desperate lives or moving to the arms of a lover, the bottle, or some other unhealthy addiction.

They meant well. They just didn't focus on the right things in life. They were very capable people who pooped out on their marriage relationship because somewhere along the line their priorities got skewed. They wanted to change, but they just couldn't find the time or energy to make it happen. Somehow they bought into the definition of insanity without ever knowing it: "Doing the same thing over and over again, hoping for a different result."

So what is getting in the way of making your marriage a top priority? Is it busyness, weariness, or a lack of replenishing relationships? How about a lack of fellowship, lack of accountability, or an unhealthy past that you are not willing to admit and do something about? Whatever is getting in the way is most likely what you will need to have the courage to face down and overcome. Sticking our heads in the sand is not a good strategy for victory!

The sad thing is that most couples actually *do know* what is holding them back; they just don't have the energy to work on it, or they place the blame on their spouse. Philosopher and author Henry David Thoreau said, "The mass of men [and women] lead lives of quiet desperation." I would add that many marriages today are not much different. We don't want to live that way, but we just don't have or take the energy to change or make it a priority. Someone once said, "Life is never kind to the areas we neglect." Far too many marriages are being neglected because we don't put in the time or have the energy to make them work.

It doesn't have to be that way! There are more than one thousand references in the Old and New Testaments telling us that *God has a plan for our lives*. His thoughts tend to go something like this: "For I know the plans I have for you," declares the Lord, "plans to prosper you and not to harm you, plans to give you hope and a future" (Jeremiah 29:11). One of the main reasons we can't find His plans for us is because we are too busy.

UNDER-CONNECTED AND OVER-COMMITTED

One of the greatest problems in America, especially in marriages and families, is this breathless pace at which we live our lives. Busyness and weariness tear down the best of marriages. A friend of mine wrote me a note once that simply read, "If the devil can't make you bad, he will make you busy." That is true! Most people are too busy and depleted to make their marriage a priority. Physical exhaustion drains the romance out of a marriage. Bill Hybels, one of the great pastors of our day, described a season of his marriage this way: "Years of fast pace and high pressure had made us both pretty awful people to live with. Our marriage seemed more like a business partnership, a joint venture, than like an intimate, loving union."[1]

When a couple is under-connected and over-committed, they begin to live their lives in *crisis mode*. They spin the plates of marriage, children, work, church, extended family, school activities, and so on. In the mix of everything else, they find less and less time to spin the marriage plate. The result? They end up in an unsatisfactory "business partnership" marriage. These kinds of relationships resemble what happens in our financial affairs. Deposits and withdrawals must be monitored carefully to guard against overdrafts in our bank accounts. In the same way, when we skimp on the important relationships in our lives, our emotional bank accounts run empty. If we take out more than we put in, our heart for God, our spouse, and our calling in life shrinks.

The sad thing about physical and emotional depletion is that it makes sincere, good people sometimes act as if they are out of their minds. Their relationships suffer and they know better, but they are just too exhausted to make a change. If you find yourself living in an under-connected, over-committed lifestyle, there are answers. They aren't necessarily easy—they'll take focus and time on our part. But what is your other option? Misery is still an option, I suppose, but I wouldn't suggest it!

In order to get back to the place of making your marriage a top priority you will have to take the necessary steps and work through some issues. You may or may not get the help you want from your spouse, but that doesn't matter at this point in your effort to create a more intimate marriage. Go ahead . . . do what it takes to make a difference in your marriage. The starting point may surprise you, though. Don't begin by focusing on your relationship. Instead, take a deeper look at your own life.

Be Ruthlessly Honest About Your Brokenness

We so often look to the other person for our happiness, but the fact is we all have some unfinished business to deal with in ourselves. Why not start there and forget about what your spouse needs to do? You won't be able to change your spouse through nagging and criticism (you've probably already tried), so you might as well start with yourself.

> **When one sinner marries another sinner, there is always going to be trouble.**

Do you have unfinished business with your parents? A past relationship? God? Did you bring expectations into your marriage, which are disappointing you right now? Is there anything you can do to repair the past? I have no doubt, unless you are a bit delusional, that an issue or perhaps many issues popped into your mind you read these questions. Remember that marriage is a *humbling journey*. When one sinner marries another sinner, there is always going to be trouble. And when these sinners have little "sinnerlings," there is even more trouble!

If you feel that your issues are too intense for you to even begin working on, or you don't know what to do, I would suggest that you seek the wisdom of a qualified marriage counselor. The Bible is clear: "Where there is no counsel, the people fall; but in the multitude of counselors there is safety" (Proverbs 11:14 NKJV). If that statement works for the entire population of Israel, then it works for your life. Some people believe that a good marriage can only be as healthy as the least healthy person in the relationship. My suggestion is to do your part to repair your own brokenness. You have nothing to lose.

One couple I know who were struggling with their marriage were adamant: neither of them would get help until the other one made the first move. They were at a stalemate and their relationship was suffering. Finally, the healthiest person in the relationship went in for counseling. As she started working on her issues, her husband became intrigued and decided to get some help himself. After working on some of their own individual problems, they began to work on their marriage. Today, they have a healthy marriage because they made their emotional and spiritual well-being a priority. Someone might ask, *What if the husband had refused to go for help?* Then the woman still would have become healthier by seeking help on her own.

A woman came up to me at a conference and was very blunt about her lack of physical intimacy with her husband. She was extremely troubled by their relationship, but as she talked more she mentioned that she had been sexually abused as a child and had not really dealt with this trauma in her life. My suggestion to her was that she would never be able to forget being victimized, so the only way to get the healing she needed was to face her fears and work through her pain. She would have wounds, but if she didn't deal with this painful part of her life, she would probably never have the marriage she hoped for.

I like how Henry Cloud describes this principle: If the tooth is infected, "pull the tooth."[2] In other words, stop the negative energy drain in your life and make room for the good stuff. The Bible says, "[There is] a time to search and a time to give up, a time to keep and a time to throw away" (Ecclesiastes 3:6). If you have been meaning to work on an issue of brokenness, then let me say that *it will never be easier than right now.* If you continue to put it off, you will only become more broken. Now is the time to do the work it takes to find wholeness for you and for your marriage. Remember, you don't have to do all of this on your own. *God created marriage, and He created the blueprint to make it work.*

Follow the Marriage Blueprint

You can't build a home (or anything else) from the wrong set of blueprints. Marriage is a God-ordained and God-sustained institution. So we need His blueprints! Frankly, I don't know how people do it without His help. While the Bible is not a marriage handbook, it does bring to light a definite strategy that works for couples. It means that we have to put aside our pride and ego and follow what Scripture says to do. The Bible is clear that we are to be *mutually submissive* to each other. I like to call this being "servant lovers."

Over the years many people have misinterpreted the Ephesians 5:22–25 passage. The word *submission* is a sticking point. Read it again, this time with fresh eyes:

> Wives, submit to your husbands as to the Lord. For the husband is the head of the wife as Christ is the head of the church, his body, of which he is the Savior. Now as the church submits to Christ, so also wives should submit to their husbands in everything. Husbands, love your wives, just as Christ loved the church and gave himself up for her.

This is a call for *mutual submission* to each other, while acknowledging that our main responsibility for submission is always directed to God. The wife is called to serve her husband, and the husband is called to serve his wife just as Christ serves the church. If every marriage had this passage as its foundation, a lot of the selfishness in marriage relationships would be dissolved.

The marriage relationship is modeled after our relationship with God. We are called to be faithful and live a life of fidelity to our spouses as well as to God. This fidelity isn't just about sexuality; it includes all aspects of life. God's relationship with Israel is a covenant relationship. This is the same kind of a relationship He asks us to make with our spouse. God's response to our failures is forgiveness, so forgiveness must be a major part of our relationship with our spouse. When we follow God's blueprints, we can't help but find a closer relationship with each other.

At most weddings, part of the love chapter (1 Corinthians 13) is quoted. Maybe the pastor read this passage of Scripture at your wedding. Take a moment to see how you measure up to the call of love in 1 Corinthians 13:4–7 (NLT):

> Love is patient and kind. Love is not jealous or boastful or proud or rude. Love does not demand its own way. Love is not irritable, and it keeps no record of when it has been wronged. It is never glad about injustice but rejoices whenever the truth wins out. Love never gives up, never loses faith, is always hopeful, and endures through every circumstance.

Two of our good friends were separated for about seven months. The issues were complicated and the tension between them was at an all-time high. I am a very positive person, and even I had little hope for the relationship. They had spent several hours with the professional counselor who had helped them through previous problems, but to no avail. They had also spent several hours with me, and we hadn't really gotten very far either.

One day they decided to meet with their pastor. Now, I believe the answer to the world's problems is found within the church, and I have the utmost respect for pastors. However, my thought was that this particular pastor didn't have the background to help with the complications of this marriage. After meeting with him, the couple called me the next day and announced, "We are moving back in together."

"Really? What happened?"

"Pastor Mark opened up the Bible and read to us some passages on how we should treat each other. All of our problems didn't go away, but we feel like we now have a handle on which direction to go."

He had read them the passages in Ephesians 5:22–33 and 1 Corinthians 13. These verses became their blueprint. They made these two passages a priority to follow, and today their marriage is better than ever. Christ loves us unconditionally and sacrificially. And He has shown us the way to love each other. Remember the WWJD bracelets that were so popular a few years ago? The commercialism perhaps killed a really powerful message. I find that when I ask the question *What would Jesus do?* regarding my marriage, I almost always get the right answer immediately. No one said it would be easy, but God did promise to walk with us through our ups and downs of life.

Personally, I am grateful for second and third and one hundredth chances in attempting to make my marriage a priority. The worries of the day and distractions of life all fight against making our marriages a priority. Just this week, as I was totally focused on writing this book, Cathy interrupted me at the computer and said, "I'm glad you are writing this book on intimacy in marriage, but when are we going to have some quality time again?" I put my papers down, took my own advice, and focused on her. It was well worth it!

MAKING YOUR MARRIAGE YOUR TOP PRIORITY

QUESTIONS FOR ME

1. If your spouse ranked your top five priorities in order of importance, what would they be?

2. What area of my life right now needs the most attention? What am I willing to do about it?

QUESTIONS FOR US

1. On a scale from 1 (needs major immediate attention) to 10 (extremely satisfied), how would you rate your relationship in the areas where you are under-connected and over-committed? Why?

Needs Attention 1 —————————— 10 Extremely Satisfied

2. What decisions could we make as a couple that would better our relationship in these areas?

The Priority Inventory

List in order the top five priorities in your life. Understanding that no one is perfect, be honest about where you are right now with your priorities.

1. _____

2. _____

3. _____

4. _____

5. _____

Now *reorder* your priorities in the way that would best honor your commitment to God and your marriage.

1. _____

2. _____

3. _____

4. _____

5. _____

Now take a moment to look at the priorities you have listed on this page. Name two priorities that you would like to work on this week, and specifically what you would do to make the necessary changes.

Priority Number One: **Priority Number Two:**

1.   1.

2.   2.

chapter 2

Creating A.W.E.* in Your Marriage

(Affection, Warmth, and Encouragement)

"We need to work on our marriage. It feels like you don't care anymore. It feels like we are settling for mediocrity, and if you would put more time and energy into our relationship we both would be in a much better place, not to mention the kids." Do those words sound familiar? I remember a day when I sort of said those words to Cathy. She had two kids in diapers and another in kindergarten. I was working too many hours and not helping as much around the house. Cathy was overwhelmed with just trying to make it through the day, and I had the audacity to say that if only *she* would make some priority adjustments we would have a more intimate marriage. Needless to say, the conversation didn't go very well. It wasn't until later in our marriage that I learned the lesson of A.W.E.

It's easy to blame your spouse for wrong priorities and lack of intimacy in your marriage. Since he or she is at least as imperfect as you, they are probably an easy target. But for this chapter I don't want you to play the "blame" game or the "if only" game. Let's focus on you and what you can do to work on the intimacy in your relationship.

You set the mood, tone, and atmosphere in your marriage. After reading this sentence some people may disagree with me, because they would blame their spouse or the needs of their children for most of the negativity in their marriage. In most cases it does take two people, but we are often quick to blame and not willing to work at setting the necessary atmosphere and attitude to create a more intimate marriage. Without sounding like a dreamer, you can change the atmosphere of your marriage almost immediately with A. W.E. (Affection, Warmth, and Encouragement). This is one of the most important lessons I have ever learned for my own marriage. Let me explain how it works.

Marsha told me that she would often greet her husband at the door with a "boatload" of problems and issues. The kids were needy, her mother was needy, work was needy, and her own health had a few issues. Marsha said that she tended to be a person who saw a glass as half empty rather than half full, and she admitted that she liked to unload her burdens on her husband whenever they entered her mind.

"How's your relationship?" I asked.

"To be honest, we aren't very close anymore. I feel like he hides from me."

"Let's try something different," I suggested. "Tonight when he comes home, keep your list of concerns to yourself. Write down all your concerns if it will help, but save those concerns for another time. Greet him with a hug and at least a fifteen-second passionate kiss. Ask about his day. Fix a good dinner. Don't bring up one solitary problem. Then see what happens. It may take a few days, but I would predict that he will hang around the kitchen, help with the meal, ask about the kids, your mother, the dog, your work, and anything else you would have brought up anyway. When he asks about your life, fill him in on what's going on, but set a *positive* tone. Keep the atmosphere upbeat. Whining and negativity are not acceptable with this experiment! Can you do that?"

She gave me a weak, "I'll try." She called me the very next day. "Jim, you will never believe what happened! I did what you suggested, as awkward as it felt to me. He just hung around the kitchen. He helped with dinner. He did the dishes with me. After dinner, instead of going straight to the television, he asked me about my day. We went out later to run an errand together and stopped at a Starbucks just to talk. Jim, you don't understand . . . that was a miracle!"

Actually, the miracle happened because Marsha took the courageous move to change the mood, tone, and atmosphere of the relationship. Will Marsha and her husband still need to confront issues and problems? Of course they will. Was her husband totally innocent as far as their problems went? Absolutely not. But *Marsha can decide* each day how to set the atmosphere in their home.

Far too many times we don't intentionally set the thermostat of our relationship to a more positive setting. Instead, we let the temperature fluctuate according to what the other person does or doesn't do. We react to the stresses of life, and the atmosphere can quickly turn negative. Let's be clear here. I didn't tell Marsha to "fake it." Her issues and needs didn't go away. She still had to deal with many of them with her husband, but *timing* is everything. Marsha needed to acquire some self-control. She tended to blurt out what was on her mind anytime she felt like it, and too often it came at the exact wrong time to get a good response. She would do it at dinner or too late at night, and then she was frustrated when her husband and her kids would try to duck the conversation or crawl into their caves.

Marsha needed to learn how to put A.W.E. into her marriage. She had to decide if she was willing to make a very courageous decision—to stop the way she had been dealing with stress in her family and set the thermostat for a "kinder, gentler atmosphere." She couldn't wait for her husband to change. She had to be the one to change the atmosphere in her marriage or it might never happen.

IT BEGINS WITH YOU AND ME

It *is* possible to have a marriage of A.W.E. and intimacy. Even with the busyness of life and all your responsibilities you can rekindle the romance and create a more intimate marriage. It is possible, but I'm not saying it will be easy. It is going to take some work and focus on your part. You can have more *affection, warmth,* and *encouragement* in any marriage, even the most high-maintenance ones, since you do have the option to set the tone and atmosphere toward greater connection and intimacy.

A.W.E. is not a Pollyanna approach to marriage. Conflict, anger, and frustration happen in the best of marriages, and in order to build true intimacy there must be moments of tension. However, far too many marriages are in poor shape because people are either not willing to work at setting a more positive atmosphere, or they are so discouraged at the lack of intimacy that they give up and take their spouse for granted.

> You won't be able to change everything about your spouse's past or the things about them that bug you.

The number of relationships trying to make it with low-level anger and years of built-up resentment is huge. It's important to realize that you won't be able to change everything about your spouse's past or the things about them that bug you. You may have to learn to live with some of his or her habits, but you can still change the atmosphere of your relationship with A.W.E.

Perhaps you identified with Marsha or her husband. You may be asking the question: "Is it even possible to improve my marriage?" You may be thinking: *We don't communicate very well, and what was once a burning, passionate relationship is now more like a business partnership within an atmosphere of tension for the purpose of managing a household of needy kids.*

If you believe the answer lies entirely within the spouse would change" department, then you might as w... this book down and look for something else. That's because *there is one person who can make a difference in your marriage atmosphere, and that one person is you.* There is no place this side of heaven where we will be free of pain, problems, frustrations, and negative people. Conflict is inevitable in relationships. However, there is a better way to deal with them, and it starts with setting an atmosphere of A.W.E. in your home.

Again, I will tell you up front, it isn't easy. It takes discipline and self-control, but I have never met anyone who has brought A.W.E. to their home relationships who has regretted it. Far too many couples live lives of quiet or not-so-quiet desperation. They are unhappy, bitter, negative people who spend most of their emotional, physical, relational, and even spiritual energy on things that won't help. The result is that they feel drained all the time instead of being full of life and vitality. I don't believe this is the way God intended for us to spend our time on planet Earth. He has a better way for us, but often we miss out. We get lazy or discouraged, or we spend all of our time blaming others. Yet we do have within ourselves what we need to create a more healthy marriage. In fact, with the right attitude we can appreciate God's abundance in our lives èven in the midst of trials and tribulations.

What if our homes were filled with less tension and more A.W.E.? What if our God-given personality was much more positive than critical? I believe it can be done, but as I mentioned, it begins with *you* making a conscious decision to bring A.W.E. into your life and relationship. You may say, "But you don't understand my life or my spouse." You are right. I don't know you, and I am blessed with a wonderful wife and family. However, a life filled with A.W.E. is a decision not to live a life based on circumstances or reactions to your spouse. It is a decision to proactively live a life filled with self-control in which you choose to set an atmosphere that leads your relationship to a healthier spot.

The Circumstances Are Irrelevant

Setting an attitude and atmosphere of A.W.E. is intentional, even in the midst of bad circumstances. One of my mentors and heroes in life was a man named Jon Campbell. Jon was a "behind the scenes" kind of guy who was extremely instrumental in the broadcast ministries of James Dobson, Chuck Swindoll, Billy Graham, Joni Eareckson Tada, Chuck Colson, Dennis Rainey, and others.

Most people who knew him forgot that he had suffered physically for a span of twenty-nine years from two bouts of Hodgkin's disease. He was told after the first bout of this cancer that he wouldn't live until Christmas of that year, but Jon chose to set the attitude and atmosphere of his life with A.W.E. He lived some of his most productive and fulfilling years, both with his work and his marriage to his wonderful wife, Peggy, after the diagnosis. He did all this while living with pain so intense that it took concentrated effort to get out of bed.

I was shocked to get a letter from him last year that read,

> Above all else, God is God. He is Holy. He is Sovereign. He is loving beyond our comprehension. He custom packages life for each of us for our good and His praise. It is within this brief yet unquestioned framework that Peg and I share the latest of what God has entrusted to' us. . . . As a result of some of my recent challenges I had an endoscope procedure last week. I'd been experiencing some difficulty in swallowing and keeping food down. The pathology came back yesterday.
>
> By God's sovereign hand, He has asked Peg and I to embrace the cancer experience a third time. I was diagnosed with adenocarcinoma-esophageal cancer. Obviously, we're a bit taken back, yet at the same time, we know every facet of our lives is to be given back to Him, with our trust and praise.

Jon and his wife, Peggy, even through difficult circumstances, chose to set the tone of their lives with an atmosphere and attitude of health, not negativity. They faced reality but at the same time kept a good and right perspective. The third time around the cancer took Jon's life, but it didn't take his spirit. Jon chose to remain a man of A.W.E. in the midst of trying circumstances. You can choose it too, no matter what life brings.

THE A.W.E. FACTOR IN MARRIAGE

In creation God said, "Let us make man in our image, in our likeness" (Genesis 1:26). We were created in the image of God. We were created to have a life with God-given *affection, warmth,* and *encouragement.* For whatever reason (and there are too many reasons and excuses to count), most couples have missed the mark. We've lost our focus. Our priorities and attitude took a wrong turn.

No one starts out to have a second-rate marriage, but it often happens because we blame our spouse and don't have the emotional energy to be intentional in making the decisions that will make a difference. When you take the time to think about it, you probably already know what you need to do. It's a matter of having the courage to change and allow God to intervene in your life.

Most people don't take the time to really examine their inner lives. Americans tend to work harder on their outside appearance than their inside soul. We scrutinize and reexamine our finances, but most of us don't take enough time to examine our lives to see how we can positively affect our marriage relationship. Many people feel dead on the inside and their relationships are stale, but they continue to function outwardly as if nothing is wrong. Below the surface, though, these ignored problems fester and break out in all sorts of negative ways. Grief that is ignored, for instance, often turns into depression and hopelessness. Hurt that is ignored becomes defensiveness toward our spouse, and suppressed anger can easily turn into bitterness. These are the tumors of our heart that can adversely affect our marriages.

TAKE THE TIME TO EXAMINE YOUR LIFE

The unexamined life lets the fast pace of our existence take over and relationships become a reaction or, worse yet, just happen. The unexamined life doesn't work at creating a life of A.W.E. or a healthy marriage. We get so distracted with emotional pain that we can't even identify the real issues. Pretty soon the negative forces of life creep inside us and before we know it, we are stale, unhappy people in poor relationships, doing things we don't want to do.

The apostle Paul's advice to Timothy was this: "Keep a close watch on yourself and on your teaching" (1 Timothy 4:16 NLT). So how can we take a closer look at ourselves and attend to the forces at work in our lives that relate to our marriage? Personally, I learn best by asking questions. Here are five questions that help me focus:

* *Is my marriage working?*

* *What's right about my marriage?*

* *What's wrong about my marriage? (And what can I do about it?)*

* *Am I giving my marriage only my emotional scraps?*

* *How can I bring A.W.E. into my marriage?*

As you create an atmosphere of A.W.E. in your marriage you will need to quit blaming your spouse, kids, parents, mother-in-law, boss, or the dog! They are not responsible for your unhappiness. Sure they may be contributing to your hurt, but unless there is abuse in your life, *you are responsible for how you respond.* My good friend Dr. Henry Cloud summarized it this way: "I cannot blame them for what I do with what they do to me. I am responsible for how I respond."[1] Given that thought, let's look at the area of affection.

A = AFFECTION

The basic need of all people is to love and be loved. So one of the basic ingredients for a marriage to thrive is affection. If you are in a marriage with very little affection, whether it's the sexual or nonsexual variety, you most likely are in a disconnected phase of your relationship. Some studies report that it takes eight to ten meaningful touches a day for a person to thrive.

> **It takes eight to ten meaningful touches a day for a person to thrive.**

You can often create an atmosphere of intimacy and closeness through affection. If you are not naturally affectionate, don't fake being overly mushy, but work on it. If your family background or ethnicity didn't offer much affection to you when you were growing up, then you'll need to make an extra effort, but don't hold back or use it as an excuse for a lack of connection in your marriage. Couples who hold hands, kiss passionately, and bring gifts like flowers and chocolate to one another are couples who have a much better chance for a healthy relationship. Back rubs work; saying "I love you" in a hundred different ways works; showing tenderness and honoring your spouse also works wonders for your relationship. Paul's advice to the Roman church was "Outdo one another in showing honor" (Romans 12:10 RSV). You may not *feel* like showering your spouse with affection. But no matter how you feel, choose to intentionally focus on bringing affection to your relationship. In most relationships you will see immediate results when you do.

Borrowing the bank analogy from the last chapter, showering your spouse with affection means placing major deposits in his or her emotional bank account. It is amazing how an empathetic hug can make all the difference in turning your relationship from negative to positive. Nagging, shaming, rudeness, irritability, and guilt won't bring connection to your relationship. Those are all *withdrawals* to your spouse's emotional bank account. Keep the emotional account full of affection so that when you take a withdrawal (and you will definitely need to at times), the account won't move to empty.

Personally, I am amazed at how often Cathy has changed my mood and the atmosphere of our home with a simple gesture of affection. One day I came home frustrated at an employee. After sharing my irritation with Cathy, instead of trying to fix it, she just gave me an extra long hug and a kiss and simply said, "I can see why that would bug you." Her affectionate response was basically saying, "I understand and I feel your pain, but now you are home and it is going to be okay."

W = WARMTH

If you haven't noticed, it really does take a lot of work, self-control, and focus to keep a relationship full of warmth. You can reset the thermostat from "chilly" to "warm," but you can't do it without an incredible amount of discipline and self-determination.

Think back to your dating days. Naturally, there was much more warmth to the relationship back then. Why? *We worked at it and we didn't feel the need to fight out every battle.* Sometimes marriages slip into bad habits, and a lack of warmth is just a bad habit. Too many relationships are trying to function with a constant low-grade anger and negative atmosphere, and that is just like trying to live life to the fullest with an infection and fever. We can function okay for a while, but eventually the temperature begins to affect us and our bodies let us down. The same thing happens when spouses live together with a lack of warmth. The marriage shuts down and moves to a lower level of fulfillment.

My mother knew how to create an environment of warmth in our home better than anyone I have ever met. Life wasn't easy for Mom. She came from a family where her father was an alcoholic and life was very difficult at times, but she had the ability to rise above her circumstances. Her favorite saying was "It's party time!" Raising four sons, working a full-time job, and keeping track of my dad kept her life filled and busy. Yet she could brighten the day of anyone with whom she came in contact, even in the midst of a stressful time.

Before she died I remember asking her how she maintained such a warm and positive spirit in the midst of her trying circumstances. Mom wasn't a particularly spiritual person, but her answer helps me every day: "I look at my life situation and I count my blessings. I can either focus on what's wrong or what's right. I choose to create an environment of love." That attitude took work and concentration on Mom's part, and she had moments when negative life issues overwhelmed her. But for the most part she decided to create a party even in the midst of trying circumstances.

Don't get me wrong. I am not saying it is possible to have a "make-believe Disneyland" type of marriage. Every marriage takes work and focus. With today's fast-paced life you can find reasons to be angry with your spouse and kids twenty-four hours a day, seven days a week, but *how is that going to help the situation?* Think warmth.

It was quite a blow to the family when my mom died. She was the "party time" person, the leader in setting the warmth of a positive atmosphere in our home. On the way to her funeral, Cathy, our three daughters, and I stopped at a flower store to pick up three long-stemmed roses. The girls wanted to place them on her casket. As we walked into the store we all noticed a bright and beautiful balloon with the words "It's Party Time!" We looked at each other and said, "This was meant to be!" We bought the balloon. We had already told the florist that we were in her store to buy flowers for a funeral. She must have thought we had a screw loose in our brains, but she didn't know my mom! I got out of the car at her graveside funeral filled with grief but carrying the "party time" balloon. As the people were gathering I went over to the casket and simply tied the balloon to it. There was a smile on all of our faces. Even in her death she was somehow reminding us that we can choose the warmth of a smile.

A friend of mine is in a high-maintenance marriage. She loves her husband, but relationships don't come easy for him. He is successful in business and often brings the tension of a high-powered job into the home. Yet I have been around them enough to know that there is a great deal of warmth in their home and relationship. I asked her how she maintains such a positive atmosphere. She replied, "I work at it. I make sure I have prayed and given my day to God. I quit whatever I am doing about fifteen minutes before he comes home. I try to have the kids in a reasonably good place. I put on soothing music. I take a few moments to at least brush my hair and then work on greeting him with warmth." She went on to say, "After a busy day at his work, it is amazing to see what a genuine smile will do for him." She works part-time herself, but she understands the power of intentionally bringing warmth to the home and the relationship.

E = ENCOURAGEMENT

The only thing that a critical spirit, nagging, and negativity bring to a relationship is lack of intimacy. Many people were raised in homes where "shame-based parenting" was the rule rather than the exception. For many, there is a natural tendency to focus on the negative side of life, but that just doesn't work in relationships. There is incredible power in encouragement and affirmation. Mark Twain once said, "I can live two months on one good compliment."

Jesus took a man named Simon and nicknamed him Peter. Peter (or *Petras*, in Greek) means "the Rock." Here was a stumbly, bumbly fisherman who kept putting his foot in his mouth, but Jesus affirmed him by believing in him. Eventually Peter did become the Rock of the early church. What changed? I believe it was the encouragement given to Simon Peter from Jesus.

Showing encouragement involves being available to your spouse. Cathy is probably busier than I am with all the details of her life, but when she stops what she is doing, even for a moment, and focuses on me, what a difference it makes. I like to take our dog for walks. There are times when I know that Cathy has already been to the gym and she has a stack of work on the table, but when she stops what she is doing and is available to walk with me even for a few minutes it really gives me a lift.

All people are drawn to encouragement and flee from negativity. Your presence in your spouse's life makes a difference. It sometimes speaks louder than words. Your availability, both physically and emotionally, says to your spouse that he or she is in a safe relationship. Don't expect to have a thriving marriage if there is too much hostility and lack of attention paid to your spouse. It just doesn't work that way. It may not be your responsibility to hound, nag, or control your spouse, but it is your God-given responsibility to encourage your spouse. Many marriages would be much better off if the spouses clearly understood that they are on the same side!

Even though I have been married to Cathy for more than thirty-one years and the most important love language for me personally is affirmation, I still have trouble at times giving the right kind of encouragement to Cathy. You will need to literally make a study of your spouse to figure out the most effective ways to encourage and affirm. Cathy appreciates complimentary words, but what she really appreciates is when I show empathy and understanding for what she is going through in life and give her help with her responsibilities.

When Cathy is overwhelmed with the workload and responsibilities of her life, the most valuable thing I can do is show empathy and encourage her by folding the clothes, cleaning up a bit, and making sure that I am taking things off her plate, not adding anything else to it. For Cathy, doing the dishes together is an affirming experience. It's not for me. I would rather "divide and conquer" our

> **Make a study of your spouse to figure out the most effective ways to encourage and affirm.**

household responsibilities. However, there are times when I have to whisper to myself, *This is not about me—it's about her!*

A.W.E. = CONTENTMENT

The result of setting an atmosphere of A.W.E. in your marriage is found in one word: *contentment*. And this is important because *contentment brings intimacy to relationships*. We live in a world where we are constantly bombarded from every angle on the promises of eternal bliss somewhere else—"the grass is always greener on the other side" mentality. Of course we know that life doesn't really work that way, especially when it comes to marital contentment.

I learned a great lesson from John Ortberg in a recent radio interview I had with him. John is one of the finest Christian communicators in the world today, and we were talking that day on my radio program about spiritual disciplines. He made a point that makes so much sense when it comes to contentment and marriage. He said, "Too many of us work on *trying* to be better instead of *training* to be better." You can *try* all you want to have a marriage of A.W.E. and intimacy, but if you don't *train* for it, then it's not going to happen.

As I have mentioned already, it takes a great deal of self-discipline and self-control to set an atmosphere of A.W.E. in your marriage. A few years ago I trained to finish the LA Marathon. (Notice I didn't say *win* the LA Marathon. Actually, I was very happy with my place of 6,487 in a group of 20,000 runners.) Since I had not run a marathon before, I asked a friend how I should train for it. He simply said, "Start running. Set a schedule with a plan and work the plan." That sounded simple enough. So I went out and bought some running shoes, wrote out a workable plan with the help of my friend, and then started the program.

The first week was easy. The second week was harder, but I completed it. Then for about the next month, I never reached my goals. I was sore and uninspired, but I had told too many people I was going to run the marathon, so I finally got back on schedule. It wasn't easy, and I definitely had some ups and downs in my preparation for the marathon. But *because I trained, I completed the goal.* If I had tried to go out and run the marathon just because it was my hope-filled goal, but didn't train, I would have never made it. This was something no one else could do for me. I had to do it myself. Today, I would say it was worth the training to accomplish the goal.

Our marriages are not that much different. If we want to have a healthy relationship, we have to put in the training and do what it takes to make it work. Despite the way Hollywood depicts intimacy, good things don't just "happen"; proper training is vital to accomplishing any goal. Contentment is a result of our proper training! Just like running a marathon, an intimate marriage takes an investment of time, energy, focus, and sometimes the help and coaching of others. It may mean something as simple as setting up daily routines that you know in the long run will produce more intimacy in the relationship. Sure there are sacrifices to make, but the result of intimacy and contentment make the effort worthwhile.

The apostle Paul understood the issue of contentment when he wrote these incredible words about his life:

> I have learned to be content whatever the circumstances. I know what it is to be in need, and I know what it is to have plenty. I have learned the secret of being content in any and every situation, whether well fed or hungry, whether living in plenty or in want. I can do everything through him who gives me strength. (Philippians 4:11–13)

For Paul, contentment was a *learned* skill. Contentment in your marriage is also a learned skill. Just like running a marathon, you have to show up every day and train. Contentment in marriage requires setting an atmosphere of A.W.E. and practicing it purposely over the long haul. Paul implies in this Scripture that contentment isn't a result of circumstances, but rather a result of an intentional lifestyle. In other words, contentment is an "inside job"—it is something we must cultivate.

Until recently I wasn't at all interested in maintaining a beautiful garden, and the crab grass and weeds in our lawn proved it. I could not have told you the name of even one single plant in our yard. However, for some reason, I have now become almost obsessed with gardening. Guess what? Our lawn and plants look much better, and I can even tell you the names of most of the tropical plants we have in the yard. What happened? I made a conscious decision to be intentional, to *work at* gardening. I developed a plan for our yard. I needed to tear out some of the old stuff and replace them in order to cultivate a beautiful garden. Just like cultivating a garden, contentment in your marriage comes from hard work and perhaps tearing out some of the old habits. It takes work and some pain. Basically, we must suffer one of two pains in our marriage: *the pain of discipline or the pain of regret.* The pain of discipline takes you on the road to a healthy marriage, while the pain of regret takes you to a dead end.

Which road are you on? Remember, problems are inevitable. Contentment in your marriage is not the result of the absence of problems. Your spouse is imperfect, your kids are imperfect, the world is imperfect, and guess what? You are also imperfect! Contentment is not determined by how many problems you face; contentment is determined by the set of your heart. The apostle Paul could write about contentment and pen the words "I can do everything through him who gives me strength" from a horrible prison cell. He acknowledged life has its problems, but he also knew that with God's help he would be given the strength to persevere.

Creating a marriage of intimacy doesn't happen overnight. That's only for Hollywood. However, the people I know who intentionally focus on setting an atmosphere of A.W.E. in their home say it is very much worth it. We will be exploring Affection, Warmth, and Encouragement in more depth in the following chapters. We will begin with one of the most effective ways to bring A.W.E. to any marriage: romance and sexual intimacy. That's where we will go next.

CREATING A.W.E. IN YOUR MARRIAGE

QUESTIONS FOR ME

1. What one thing can I do to bring more A.W.E. to my marriage relationship?

2. Answer the questions from page 44:

   * *Is my marriage working?*

   * *What's right about my marriage?*

   * *What's wrong about my marriage? (And what can I do about it?)*

   * *Am I giving my marriage only my emotional scraps?*

QUESTIONS FOR US

1. Share with each other your answers to #2 in the *Questions for Me* section.

2. In what season of your marriage did you experience the most A.W.E.?

3. What could you as a couple do to bring back more A.W.E. into your relationship?

HEART-TO-HEART HOMEWORK
DEPOSITS AND WITHDRAWALS

To bring A.W.E. and intimacy into your relationship, be sure you are making more deposits into the well-being of your spouse than withdrawals.

A *deposit* is anything positive and security-producing that gives your spouse energy. A *withdrawal* is anything sad or negative that drains energy from your spouse.

1. What are some ways you can make more deposits into your spouse's account?

2. What deposits do you wish you could receive from your spouse?

3. Identify ways you are taking withdrawals from your spouse's account. What action steps can you immediately take to reduce them?

Affection, Romance, and Intimacy

If someone would have told Cathy and me before we were married that we would have to work at our sexual relationship, I think we would have laughed at them. With hormones running at breakneck speed it didn't dawn on us until later that our sexual relationship would take work and intentionality, and that we would literally be developing our sexual intimacy over the years.

Contrary to what Hollywood wants us to believe, sex is not just an event or individual acts of intimacy. It involves much more. It is important to set an atmosphere of A.W.E. in this area so you can work toward a closer and more fulfilling relationship. If you need help in this area, get it. Obviously, it is best if you and your spouse are on the same page with your desires, wants, hopes, and prayers for your relationship. However, even if you are feeling alone in this, you can make dramatic progress by simply being proactive about your sexual relationship.

Sex is not about an event; it is about creating a positive, romantic, healthy, sexually intimate environment. You can set the tone and the atmosphere of your sexual relationship to be more affectionate, and even the stalest of relationships will change dramatically almost immediately. Here is a verse of Scripture I quoted in chapter 2 that seems to fit as a preface to this chapter on sexuality: "Outdo one another in showing honor" (Romans 12:10 RSV).

Just like I tell students at a youth rally, sex is so much more than "doing it." Sex was created by God, and it is designed to be fun, serious, sacred, and pleasurable. Sex is closely related to communication, and it frankly takes work on both sides to experience it fully. Even after thirty-one years of marriage, Cathy and I are still learning about our sexual relationship.

After giving a very frank talk on this subject at a retreat I was speaking at, a woman came up to me and said, "I feel physically and emotionally abandoned by my husband. We are active in our church, successful in business, and busy with raising our children, but the romantic side of our relationship is almost nil. We do periodically have a sexual relationship, but most nights we lay within six inches of each other but are emotionally and sexually miles apart."

She is not the only person who feels like that. The sad fact is, if the majority of people were brutally honest about their relationship they would say the same thing. My experience tells me that if a couple is not growing *together* physically and emotionally then they are probably growing *apart*. We were created by God to connect sexually with our spouse, no matter what season of marriage we are in. That connecting may look different at different ages and stages of our lives, but that doesn't mean it ceases to be important.

Let's start at the beginning. God created our sexuality, and from a spiritual perspective, sex between a husband and wife symbolizes the most important relationship you have on earth. Jesus quoted part of the creation account when He responded to a question about marriage.

> Haven't you read . . . that at the beginning the Creator "made them male and female," and said, "For this reason a man

will leave his father and mother and be united to his wife, and the two will become one flesh"? So they are no longer two, but one. Therefore what God has joined together, let man not separate. (Matthew 19:4–6)

The symbolism is so graphic. When a man and woman are joined together, they literally become one flesh. There isn't a better illustration of becoming "united" or "one flesh" than coming together in sexual union. Far too many couples have had so many negative statements thrown at them about sexuality, sometimes from their childhood, that they have forgotten that our sexuality, in the beauty of a marriage, is a gift from God. We are called to enjoy it, and grow our relationship closer through it.

> **Our sexuality, in the beauty of a marriage, is a gift from God.**

Scripture doesn't discuss a marriage relationship without a physical union. The beautiful, somewhat erotic imagery of a sexual relationship between husband and wife is found in several passages in the Bible. In Genesis we learn that Adam *knew* his wife, Eve. The Hebrew idea *to know* is actually expressing the completeness and intimacy of a God-honoring sexual and emotional relationship. A marriage can't be based solely on sex. But a marriage can't be devoid of sexuality either. God created the mystery of the sexual relationship and said, "It is very good." When a couple understands the sacredness of their sexual relationship they can bring A.W.E. to their emotional relationship as well.

DEVELOPING SEXUAL INTIMACY

One of the major themes of this book is that *we must be intentional* about our marriage relationship. I wish I had a hundred dollars for every couple who has expressed to me at one time or another that they haven't taken the time to develop a plan or even communicate their needs because they thought the other person should just figure it out on their own. If that is your attitude—and nothing can change your mind—then skip this part of the book, because even with sexual intimacy we need a plan and we need to work at it or it just won't happen. There is a better way; here are some key ingredients to developing sexual intimacy in your marriage.

GIVE SEXUAL INTIMACY THE TIME AND ATTENTION IT DESERVES

If you are too tired to work on your sexual intimacy, then you have your priorities in the wrong place. If you feel overworked, overtired, and underappreciated then you are the one who can take some positive steps to change. Remember, I didn't say this was going to be easy! The breathless pace of life most Americans are living is one of the strongest deterrents of a fulfilled life. Each day I have to ask myself this question: "Am I giving Cathy only my emotional scraps?"

Far too many people give out so much with all the other needs around them that they have nothing left when it comes to building romance and creating A.W.E. in their marriage. Often we want our spouse to change or "take over" the romance department. But since you are the one reading this book, the odds are that it will be *you* who will have to be proactive, or nothing is going to change. If nothing changes it is very possible that your romantic relationship and sexual intimacy will become even more stale.

My friends Terry and Jennifer were living life at a pace way too fast. They both had good intentions and a full plate of wonderful activities for their kids, church, school, and work. These were great people who loved life and were committed to their marriage. Their kids were preteens and teens, and life was busy with activities and more activities. As they talked to me they told me they were just beginning to become aware that their marriage was in a "very unfulfilling stage."

I was getting tired just *listening* to their schedule and the demands on their life. Terry and Jennifer then opened up to me, sharing that at one time they had a fulfilling, sexually intimate relationship, but now both were deeply disappointed by the lack of passion in their marriage. They were still committed to each other, but they felt more like roommates in a business relationship than a married couple.

Here is what I asked them: "Are you willing to work on your sexual intimacy?" They laughed, and then when they saw that I was serious, they said, "Sure."

My next question surprised them. "What are you willing to *give up* to proactively work on this on a regular basis?" You see, their lives were too full and they were simply too tired to take on one more responsibility in their already overcrowded schedule. "Do you have a regular date night?"

"No."

"How often do you go away and just focus on each other?"

"Not very often."

"Do you have time in your weekly schedule to spend at least two hours on romance and intimacy?" They looked at each other with blank stares before turning back toward me. I think I remember saying, "I feel your pain!" But in my heart I knew that *if they were too tired to work on their sexual intimacy something was very wrong.* These were people who didn't need me to make them feel guilty, and I surely didn't have to convince them that sexual intimacy was a worthwhile lifelong pursuit for their relationship. They simply—or better yet, not so simply—needed to cut back and do less so that they could have more time to focus on each other.

The Passion Plan

If you feel like Terry and Jennifer, here's my prescription. I'm not saying it is easy to do, but I've never met anyone who has followed this prescription tell me it wasn't worth it. I call it the *Passion Plan.* Putting the words "passion" and "plan" together may not sound very romantic, but the plan works. Frankly, I am not one who believes in simple little techniques and formulas that will magically turn your marriage around, but this really works! And it works because of the time and energy it takes for you to focus on your sexual intimacy.

You will need to reserve at least:

15 seconds a day
15 minutes 5 days a week
1.5 hours a week
And another 1.5 hours a week

I am no math major, but this adds up to four hours, sixteen minutes, and forty-five seconds. I do realize that is a great deal of time in an already overcommitted schedule, but what are the other options? My good friend Henry Cloud wrote a great book called *9 Things You Simply Must Do*. One of the nine things was "Play the movie." Here's what he meant by this: We have to ask the question, *What will happen in the end?* Henry says, "Playing the movie means never to see any individual action as a singular thing in and of itself" but rather "any one thing you do is only a scene in a larger movie. To understand that action, you have to play it out all the way to the end of the movie."[1]

Are the choices you are making today about your sexual intimacy going to be harmful or helpful to your relationship in the years to come?

Here is my question to you. Are the choices you are making today about your sexual intimacy going to be harmful or helpful to your relationship in the years to come? Let's face it, far too many couples find themselves empty nesters and empty of romance at the same time. So *now* is the time to work on the relationship, not at divorce court or years from now. Here's the Passion Plan.

1. Kiss passionately for at least 15 seconds every day.

Daily passionate kissing keeps the fire burning. This is not about sex; it is about intimacy. Some women don't want to kiss passionately because they are afraid it will lead to sex . . . and that isn't what they desire at the moment. I agree that can be a problem. But it doesn't have to be seen as simply a precursor to having sex.

A passionate kiss before you leave for work leaves a fresh aroma of feelings throughout the day. A passionate kiss when you see each other after a long day apart may be more intimate than anything else you could do to keep the romantic fires burning. Couples who don't kiss passionately often feel sexually and emotionally abandoned. Kissing is personal, and it is often a good indication of the quality of your marriage relationship. When there is even a short time of passionate kissing each day you will be much more likely to have a satisfying sexual relationship. I read somewhere recently that one prostitute told her clients, "I will have sex with you, but *I will not kiss you.* Kissing is far too intimate."

Passionate kissing, even for just fifteen seconds, releases feelings about each other that say, "I love you; I want to be with you; you are special to me." Obviously there are days in any relationship when we feel angry, resentful, or frustrated. My suggestion is to take a moment to still do the fifteen-second passionate kiss. It won't make your problems go away. You will still need to deal with them. However, you are telling each other that *"no matter what is happening I still find you attractive and I am willing to work on our relationship."* One last thought: There's no rule that you have to keep it at fifteen seconds. Go ahead and splurge . . . go for longer!

2. Take 15 minutes at least 5 days a week to connect and talk.

Frankly, if there is no emotional intimacy or connection, there will be very little interest in sexual intimacy. If you don't have time to talk, you won't have time to have much physical intimacy either. Find a time each day to connect. Leave your problems at work, school, or church, and even put aside your children's issues for a few minutes, and focus only on each other. Hold hands while you talk. Close your door and make sure the kids know that you are taking your fifteen-minute time just for you.

Cathy and I like to go for a walk with the dog around our neighborhood or at the beach near where we live. Find something you can do with your spouse that you both enjoy. This is not the time to bring up the heavy issues. It is a time to check in and hear about the day, share thoughts, and anything that happened that you have been waiting to communicate. *Focus on each other.* Make sure you are offering words of affirmation to your spouse every day, even when you aren't in the mood to do so. Try to intentionally refresh each other with your fifteen minutes together. Don't drain the other person. Make sure there are more deposits in your love accounts than withdrawals in your fifteen-minute connection. This will make both of you more excited about coming back together each day.

For most of us this will probably feel awkward at first, but with A.W.E. being sown into our relationship regularly it will get comfortable very quickly. You will need to focus on self-control. Otherwise, you'll end up not connecting positively but immediately moving to areas of conflict or sharing burdens during this time. This is not the time to bring up conflict! Keep focused on creating A.W.E. and seeing your intimacy grow as a result. Of course you need to share burdens at times, and you will take withdrawals from your spouse, but don't use these fifteen minutes that way. This is time set aside to *energize* your relationship.

I was thinking about this the other day when Cathy and I were on a walk. What I felt she needed at the time was empathy. She didn't need me to fix her problems. She needed me to simply identify with her that life wasn't easy in this season of her life. I said, "I was praying for you this morning, and I once again realized what an amazing amount of weighty burdens you are carrying on your shoulders." I then mentioned them—her best friend was critically ill (she later died), her mother was extremely needy (Cathy is definitely in the "sandwich" generation of still dealing with kids and now dealing with a parent), our church had experienced a horrible split that caused Cathy a great amount of grief, and so on. It was a long list of challenges.

There was nothing I could do to change what had happened to her in the past year, and little I could do to change what was presently going on. She just needed to know that *I recognized* her season of extra stress and pain. It was a meaningful time of connection because empathy is a powerful connector. If your spouse is struggling with something at work, a family issue, or maybe a health problem, take the time to connect and show authentic empathy. Sure, there will be times of stress and intense discussions, but try not to have them during your fifteen-minutes-a-day connection time.

3. Date and court your spouse for at least 1.5 hours a week.

As I mentioned in the chapter on priorities (chapter one), a nonnegotiable, regularly scheduled date night (or day or morning) is one of the most effective ways for couples to stay connected. For most of us, our lives are highly scheduled anyway. So why is it difficult to schedule a date with our spouse on a weekly basis?

Money doesn't have to be an excuse, because you can have a date with no money. Some of Cathy's and my favorite dates are out in nature or doing things that don't cost much. If you can't afford a baby-sitter and you need one, then trade date times with another couple. Be sure to save some of your energy from the rest of your day so when you go out on your date you have the energy to focus on your spouse. My guess is that before you were married you reserved some of your best energy for your dates. Reserve some of that energy for your date night and watch your marriage be filled with more A.W.E. Your weekly date is not the time for taking care of family business or personal problems. It's not the time to emote and do a dump of all that is going on in your life. Focus on relating to your spouse. Enjoy each other's company with an emphasis on romance. As the old commercial says, "Try it—you'll like it." Now for the last 1.5 hours.

4. Schedule into your life 1.5 hours a week for sexual intimacy.

If you are like most people you might stumble on the word *schedule*. Spontaneity is wonderful when it comes to romance, and I wish for you many breathtaking, spontaneous moments. But all authorities will tell you that a weekly scheduled time for romance is anything but boring. (It can be more often than once a week, of course, but once a week is a good place to start.) You schedule doctor's visits, dates, business appointments, and the kids' activities. So go ahead and schedule 1.5 hours a week for an important time of building intimacy. I would suggest you actually put it on your calendar. That way, you can both look forward to it.

At first it may seem a bit mechanical, but after a few scheduled "appointments," you will most likely look forward to this treasured time together. The reason I put down 1.5 hours (besides trying to be cutesy with the numbers 1 and 5 theme) is because if you take the time to focus on each other sexually, you will tend to be much more romantic since you won't feel rushed. Why not try candles, a bubble bath, and back rubs, really taking time to focus on each other? Schedule your sexual intimacy for once a week and then watch to see if it doesn't happen more often, with more spontaneity than you have ever had before.

"It's Wednesday!"

I know a couple who schedule sex every Wednesday. He is a pastor of a fairly large church and she is busy as a homemaker, Bible study teacher, and chief taxi driver of their five preteen and teenage kids. Needless to say, life is full and their house can be a zoo. Why they chose Wednesday I have no idea, but every Wednesday night the kids are put to bed at a decent time and out come the candles and romance.

Oftentimes they wake up in the morning and the first words out of their mouths are *"It's Wednesday!"* My friend tells me that a Wednesday rarely goes by without an email from his wife that simply says: "It's Wednesday!" Believe it or not, most weeks he speaks at a mid-week church service on Wednesday evening. There are times when his wife, who is often sitting next to him, will whisper in his ear during the service, "It's Wednesday!" I asked him if that ever distracts him. He just laughed and said, "People appreciate that I am never long-winded on Wednesday nights!" Obviously their secret is not announced to anyone. I don't live in the same state, but I guarantee you that I have never called them on a Wednesday night!

Does the scheduling of romance ever become a burden? Not really. It is usually something couples look forward to. Of course there are nights when they don't take the entire 1.5 hours, and other times when they have to postpone because someone is sick or out of town. But the idea is to *prioritize romance*. So pick a day and see if this advice isn't worth the entire price of this book.

BE WILLING TO RUTHLESSLY WORK ON THE THINGS THAT HOLD YOU BACK FROM SEXUAL INTIMACY

Before you call all of this "Pollyanna" talk, please know that I do not believe that you should repress your conflicts or the issues in your marriage. I just don't think that in order to develop a marriage of A.W.E., you can afford to let your problems leak out on every situation or at any time. *Negativity is a drain on romance*, so find an appropriate time and place to work on whatever is holding you back as a couple from experiencing a deepened sexually intimate relationship.

If you have anger and resentment toward each other, do what it takes to work on the issues fueling that. In today's fast-paced, stress-filled society we can usually find reasons to be angry at our spouse twenty-four hours a day, seven days a week. When we don't deal with the issues, we become emotionally distant, and that always causes struggles with physical intimacy.

Once when I was talking about this subject to an audience, a woman came up to me and said, "What if I always feel overworked, overtired, and underappreciated?"

My reply was "I think most people feel that way, and that's why most people rate their romantic relationship with their spouse as below their hopes or expectations." The question I would ask you is: Who is most responsible for that woman's feelings of being overworked, overtired, and underappreciated? Is it her not-very-sensitive husband, or is it her? Obviously it involves both of them. Unfortunately for her, she didn't seem to be getting the attention she needed from her husband. But as we talked more, it became clear that her feelings were mostly being fueled by choices *she* was making.

It seems that most of her life was spent in "crisis mode," managing a very busy household with pretty much no time for her own care. She resented her husband for not coming alongside her more often and was frustrated with her children because they didn't seem to be helping enough either. Did she have an easy situation? No, she didn't. She admitted that her crisis-mode living was causing her to be irritable, and she knew her husband and children spent some of their time "ducking" (avoiding) her.

Here's my advice to her: "You will need to ruthlessly eliminate stress in your life. I urge you to cut back and do less." She said nothing but the look on her face was *But you don't understand.*

I said, "This isn't going to be easy for you, is it?"

She responded, "Not easy—and probably impossible. I just need *help* from my family." She went on to describe her life of work, exhaustion, under-appreciation, and pressure.

I asked, "What areas of your life can you cut back your responsibilities and do less?" She couldn't come up with a single area! I then had to tell her that she would remain overworked, overtired, and underappreciated. And, frankly, she was putting her entire marriage in jeopardy. None of it registered.

Two years later her husband had an extramarital affair. Their marriage was lost. I honestly think they could have saved the marriage if some radical surgery to their schedule had been done as soon as the warning signs began to appear. Wasn't it Jesus who said, "What profit is it to a man if he gains the whole world, and loses his own soul?" (Matthew 16:26 NKJV). This couple lost the soul of their marriage because they weren't willing to ruthlessly cut out parts of their busy schedule and find time for romance with each other. If you feel your own marriage is going down that avenue, then please do whatever it takes to focus on each other. Soccer practice and a cleaner house can wait.

CREATE AN ENGEDI FOR YOUR SEXUAL INTIMACY

Most people have heard of the word Engedi, but can't put their finger on where or what it is. Engedi is one of the most beautiful spots in all of Israel. It is cool water in the heat of a barren land. It is a hidden, private sanctuary with the sweet smell of flowers and the breathtakingly beautiful backdrop of exotic birds and animals in the midst of a dry desert. It is where King David fled to get away from Saul. It is an oasis in the midst of a lifeless desert.

King Solomon wrote a very candid and beautiful illustration of sexual intimacy in the book of the Bible entitled Song of Solomon, or Song of Songs. As he describes a rather erotic scene in the beginning of the book he mentions Engedi. "My beloved is to me a cluster of **God wants your sexual relationship to be an oasis of refreshment and beauty for you and your spouse.** henna blooms in the vineyards of En Gedi" (Song of Solomon 1:14 NKJV). God wants your sexual relationship to be an oasis of refreshment and beauty for you and your spouse. In order to accomplish this, you need to find your oasis in your relationship with your spouse. There is nothing dirty about creating your sexual Engedi.

An Engedi experience doesn't happen when couples do the typical . . . climb into bed, kiss, cuddle, have sexual intercourse, and in eight minutes are fast asleep. Engedi experiences take preparation and are worth the time and energy invested. Each couple needs to find what suits them best, but most of the couples I know who proactively work on their sexual relationship will *take time to prepare* for their special sexual encounter. If the average man came home with flowers, made sure the bedroom didn't have laundry all over it, took care of the kids, lit some candles, showered, drew a bubble bath for his wife, and then left her alone for half an hour in the tub with soft music coming out of their stereo, I don't think they would have a problem with a beautiful sexual encounter that evening!

One couple told me that to celebrate special occasions they send the kids over to Grandma's house (or get them to bed early) and then they give each other a half-hour massage. Since both of them love a massage, they gave each other the gift of taking a class together at the local community college. For them, a relaxing massage is a sure way of creating their Engedi.

In 1 Samuel 24:1, Engedi is mentioned as David's stronghold, a safe place where he and his men hid from their enemy. In the same way, your Engedi must be a safe, intimate stronghold, an oasis in the desert of life. *Engedi is a place of renewal.* Your physical needs are satisfied, but it is also a place where your emotional and spiritual needs are met as well. Revive one another and your marriage in the streams of your own Engedi.

When you decide to make sexual intimacy a priority in your life, you and your spouse will be more physically connected, but you will become more emotionally connected as well. Don't wait for your spouse to initiate this plan; let the initiation begin with you. You can buy the candles and turn your bedroom into an Engedi. Your spouse will be pleasantly surprised, and as time goes on will look forward to this special time of connection as much as you do.

AFFECTION, ROMANCE, AND INTIMACY

QUESTIONS FOR ME

1. Here's what I can do to bring more affection, warmth, and intimacy to my marriage.

2. If I could talk to an expert on sexual intimacy, I would ask this question:

QUESTIONS FOR US

1. From this chapter, brainstorm ideas you can introduce to each other that will bring more affection, romance, and intimacy to your relationship.

2. If there was one thing I could do to bring you joy this week, what would it be?

HEART-TO-HEART HOMEWORK

1. Planning an Engedi Experience
   Plan an "almost perfect" romantic time together and then set a time in the very near future to experience your own Engedi.

2. Brainstorm

What would this special time look like?

Look at your calendar and schedule this date—the sooner the better. When?

Communication: A Key to Warmth in Your Marriage

The trait that is most closely linked to the success or failure of your marriage is your ability to communicate. Marriage authorities don't always agree on issues, but I have never heard of even one who doesn't say that most marriages derail primarily because of inadequate communication. Over the years I have had the privilege of doing hundreds of premarital sessions with couples. I always ask, "How's your communication?" No one has ever said anything but "Great! We talk about everything."

At their six-month after-marriage checkup I ask the same question, and in the vast majority of cases communication is already one of the main issues they want to talk about because they are having problems. Our goal with a marriage of A.W.E. is intimacy. We want to be emotionally and physically connected in an intimate way. But in many marriages poor communication habits prevent that from happening.

Most couples didn't have good role models growing up.

When you combine a lifetime of unhealthy communication habits and poor conflict-resolution skills, you hurt your chances of experiencing true intimacy. Add to that the many different styles of communication, and it is no wonder people regularly struggle in this area.

If you want to intimately connect with your spouse, you will need to roll up your sleeves and work at bettering your communication. It's important to remember that before warmth and freedom can come to a damaged relationship, there might be some pain in the process. We all want a marriage where there is warmth and connectivity, but most people aren't willing to work at the relationship enough to bring the marriage to a more positive place. Before we look at how to enhance communication with your spouse, we need to look at what keeps you from communicating and connecting effectively.

CONFLICT AND COMMUNICATION

Keep your goal in mind—affection, warmth, and encouragement (A.W.E.) in an intimately connected relationship. (At least most of the time!) You are not alone if your marriage has gotten bogged down in the daily monotony of doing life together. Taking a vow to marry that special person and then trying to raise PG children in an R-rated world is anything but boring. Interestingly enough, though, it can become *mundane*. This happens when we don't work at settling our conflicts and we live with huge amounts of low-level anger, resentment, and lack of respect.

As soon as we begin to take each other for granted or expect the worst from each other, we are making major strides toward killing the A.W.E. in our relationship. Conflict and problems will come into any healthy relationship. It's not a matter of *if* they will be a part of your relationship; the only thing to be determined is *how* this conflict will affect your relationship. The often-quoted statement attributed to Martin Luther works here: "We cannot keep the birds from flying over our heads, but we do not have to let them build nests in our hair."[1] If your marriage suffers from a lack of warmth, then take a serious look at some of the traps that can put extra tension in a marriage and seek to avoid them.

OVER-COMMITMENT AND PHYSICAL EXHAUSTION

All of us are much more likely to fight, get defensive, and say the wrong thing at the wrong time when we are physically depleted. Sure there are seasons of a marriage when the physical demands on our bodies are more intense. It just comes with the territory. Handling new babies, toddlers, and taking on more work often brings physical deprivation. If we are in these situations for too long without some relief, we begin to see the deprivation as normal, and that can be damaging to the marriage relationship. When people are "dangerously tired" their communication skills weaken.

Tom and Terri came into my office one day to talk about their teenage son who was experimenting with marijuana. They needed answers, and they hoped I could help. When they walked into my office, they both looked *totally exhausted*. I asked about their life. Both worked more than full time. They said the house payments and car payments were killing them. They were juggling home responsibilities, church life, the kids' activities, and at least one sick parent. Their financial debt was smothering them, and the stress of the teenage years had not been kind to their relationship with their son and daughter.

After hearing their story for just a few minutes, I was exhausted! Before we talked about their son's marijuana problem, I asked, "How's your relationship with each other?"

They looked blankly at me, and Terri said, "What relationship?"

Those two words spoke volumes. I could already feel the tension between them. Reading into her statement told me they were sacrificing their marriage relationship for the "joy" of raising two kids, dealing with a sick parent, making those huge mortgage payments, and acquiring all the other trappings of success.

At the risk of sounding trite, I knew there was no way they were going to make much of a difference in their son's life if they didn't do some radical surgery on their marriage and lifestyle. You may identify with this couple. If you are in the same situation, you may even be thinking, *There really is nothing I can change.*

I surprised them by saying, "I don't think I can help you. I would hate to add one more responsibility to your already overcrowded life."

They looked at me with great disappointment. The husband hesitated before asking: "What would you do?"

I smiled and shook my head. "You're not going to like my answer."

He was a straight shooter and responded, "Go ahead, give us your best shot."

> **Nothing changes until the pain of remaining the same is greater than the pain of changing.**

This is basically what I said to them: "Here is my quote of the day: Nothing changes until the pain of remaining the same is greater than the pain of changing."[2]

They asked, "What does that mean?"

I replied, "In the fifteen minutes we have been talking, you both have told me that you are exhausted from work and other responsibilities. Your son is experimenting with risky drug use, and you are under a heavy debt load. You said your own relationship is more like roommates than husband and wife because you are so focused on just getting through the day. You mentioned that there is very little margin in your life for communication and intimacy."

They nodded in agreement. "Keep going," the husband interjected.

"Okay, I will! You seem over-committed and under-connected with each other and with your children. A business success or a business failure can take the energy out of well-meaning intentions. I would say most of your time and energy is going into your business and you are giving your family—especially your marriage—only your emotional scraps. You mean well, but I have to ask you: Is it working at home? It was that great theologian of the Green Bay Packers, Coach Vince Lombardi, who said, 'Fatigue makes cowards of us all.' I am by no means calling you a coward, but I know when I am as tired as you both look, I am a lousy husband to Cathy and a lousy parent to my children. Fatigue sucks the life out of our best intentions, causing us to make major relational mistakes. The incredibly long hours you both focus on work and other responsibilities means you have little time to invest in your primary relationships: God, your marriage, your children, replenishing friendships, and even the health of your own bodies. Healthy communication takes time, courage, energy, and effort. I wish I had an easy answer for you, but I can only offer difficult and complicated decisions."

I then recommended that they take a weeklong, do-nothing vacation and ask themselves the question, "What would it take to reprioritize our lives for healthier communication?" I told them that they might not like the answers, but I was confident that they could come up with the solution to their communication crisis.

They sat for a while, a bit stunned. Like all of us, they were looking for a *quick fix*. But two weeks later they took that vacation with their children. They spent time reconnecting and reevaluating. They communicated in ways that they had not, as a couple or a family, for many years. They made bold financial decisions. They looked at their relationship with their kids, especially their relationship with their son who was doing drugs. They realized that it was a very short season of time before he would be out on his own. They played the tape forward and didn't like what they saw. So they began the process of making the hard decisions to cut back.

Terri moved to part-time work, they sold the cars to get out of big payments, and bought used cars. They made a decision to try to have dinner together as a family at least five times a week. Tom and Terri decided to rigorously protect their weekly date night and created a plan to do some radical surgery on their family and marriage priorities.

Two years later, I now put this family on my "hero list." Both Terri and Tom work less hours, communicate more, and spend quality time with the rest of their family. They would say *the difficult decisions were worth the effort and sacrifice.* One of the good results of putting some margin back in their life is that their son hasn't tried drugs again, not even once.

No one said it would be easy, but making changes to your schedule may be the best decision you can make to keep an atmosphere of warmth, connectivity, and healthy communication flowing in your family. I am not suggesting that the decisions they made are the answers for every couple who find themselves over-committed and under-connected. Obviously, adjustments need to be made that suit each couple's situation. Sometimes the changes need to be dramatic (like in Terri and Tom's life) and other times just a bit of fine-tuning will make the difference.

Unfortunately, there are other traps to watch for as well.

DEFENSIVENESS DESTROYS INTIMACY

Defensiveness is another barrier to connection and good communication with your spouse. It destroys positive conversation and intimacy, making healthy communication virtually impossible. Research shows that a defensive communication attitude rarely has the effect we desire. In many ways, defensiveness is another way of blaming our spouse. When people are defensive, it is usually because their emotional needs are not being met. They do not feel safe or accepted by their spouse. Their healthy self-esteem is being threatened and so they lash out with defensiveness.

When I am defensive with Cathy or when she is defensive with me, we have to ask: "What is the story *behind* the story?"

For me, it is usually unresolved conflict or low-level anger about something else. For Cathy, it is often simply exhaustion. At other times it's a hurt from her past sometimes tied to the way she grew up as a child.

When defensiveness arises, we have to ask these questions: *What is making me so insecure? Why am I angry? Hurt? Disappointed? Shamed? Sad? Is there another emotion that is crippling our connection?* In my case, it often takes time to figure out what emotion is at work in me. Most of us are so good at stuffing our emotions that we find it very difficult to immediately figure out what we are feeling.

> **Most of us are so good at stuffing our emotions that we find it very difficult to immediately figure out what we are feeling.**

A common reaction is to withdraw and crawl into our relational "cave." I am prone to that reaction. I have mentioned to Cathy on more than one occasion, "I know I look cool and calm on the outside, but I am screaming on the inside." On the other hand, another common reaction when we are feeling defensive is to yell, scream, and verbally attack our spouse and kids. The screamer is often dealing with many other emotional issues besides the conflict at hand. Neither way of communicating is healthy, and frankly, neither works to bring about connection or intimacy. This seems obvious to most people, but our vulnerable emotional health can get in the way of rationality. Even though we know we shouldn't, we still find ourselves communicating with a defensive attitude.

What pattern of communication do you turn to when you are feeling defensive and vulnerable? I can think of four styles that we most often adopt. They won't help you connect, but most of us revert to one or more of these styles when we get defensive.

1. *Withdrawal:* These are the crawl-into-a-cave people. They might pout, or they might simply refuse to engage in any communication. Sometimes they change the focus of the conflict by

literally walking away from it and spending their emotional energy on work, the house, the kids, or anything that will keep them out of the conflict with their spouse.

2. *Aggression*: These are the screamers. They are loud and angry. They use threats, manipulation, or control to "win."

3. *Passivity*: These are the whiners. They are people who feel victimized and they blame others for what is happening to them. They have an inability to say no, even when saying yes may hurt communication in the long run.

4. *Assault*: These people communicate by throwing fits of rage. They have been known to be destructive to property and even their spouse by hitting, kicking, and throwing objects.

All four of these styles of communication are negative, and in a way are forms of being defensive because the person's emotional health is not in a good place. The communication traps just keep coming. The next one is especially difficult and destructive.

ADDICTS DON'T DO INTIMACY

There is nothing like an addiction of any kind to stifle good communication and block intimacy. During a time when Steve Arterburn and I wrote the book *Drug-Proof Your Kids*, I spent a great deal of time working with drug abusers, alcoholics, and their families. What always amazed me was how so many of these addicts were incredible people, and some were highly successful in their businesses. The vast majority had good intentions. However, one thing they all had in common was that *they were leaving a trail of broken relationships along the path of their self-destruction.*

I remember one day in particular. I was chatting with a group of men who were residing at a rehabilitation center and had been sober for several weeks. After listening to their stories, I finally blurted out to them, "Addicts don't do intimacy very well!" The more we talked, the more we realized that it's not only the addicts, but the entire family who struggles with intimacy and communication. No matter what the addiction is, the result is the same: poor communication, lack of intimacy, destructive behaviors, and broken relationships.

If you or your spouse is an addict, then know two things. First, there is help for you. Millions of addicts have overcome their destructive behavior. You must have an intense desire to get the help you need, but the answers to your problems are available. Second, if you don't get the help you need and make the necessary changes, you will *never* find healthy communication and the kind of intimacy I am talking about in this book. If your experimentation with anything (pornography, gambling, alcohol, drugs, and even compulsive eating) is showing you that you are powerless over this addiction, then be aware of what the ultimate result will be. It *could* be physical death, but it will *most likely* be the death of your marriage unless you seek help.

Bob and Linda were in what some would call a "functionally dysfunctional" marriage. Both were successful in their careers, active in church, and seemed to get along with others well. Both were functioning alcoholics. (Only 5 to 10 percent of alcoholics ever make it to skid row. Most work alongside you, attend your churches, or are your neighbors.) As the story so often goes with an addict, Bob not only had a problem with drinking but pornography as well. He was filled with shame, but kept thinking he could beat his problems on his own. Linda drank to numb her pain, both from her broken relationship with Bob and the effects of a dysfunctional home growing up.

Finally Bob got caught with some very embarrassing pornography on his computer, and his life unraveled. *This may have been the best thing that could have happened to him, because when he hit rock bottom he sought help.* He started attending a men's group at his church where he was brutally honest. He became absolutely focused on getting well, and this caused him not only to attend the men's group but also Alcoholics Anonymous and a weekly meeting for those with sex addictions. Bob took on a Christian sponsor and worked his program. Today Bob is healing.

Linda, on the other hand, kept right on drinking. Even

though Bob was becoming a much healthier person, Linda still didn't get the help she needed. Bob lost sixty pounds; he began a regimen of working out physically and spiritually. He quit focusing on Linda's problems and got the help he needed for himself. Finally, after some very frustrating years, Linda followed Bob and began to move toward health and healing.

If they had not swallowed their pride and reached out for help, their marriage would be long over and they would still be facing a boatload of other problems. There is hope for addicts, but they must take two very important steps. First, they must admit that they are powerless over their addiction. Then they must seek God's help and the help of people who know the answers.

If you are an addict, it will be very difficult to work on your communication and intimacy issues before you deal with your addictions. So seek the help you need in this area without delay. Addictions aren't the trap for everyone though. The next trap we'll look at may be the most destructive of all.

NEGATIVITY AND SHAME-BASED COMMUNICATION

This is a trap that stifles intimacy over time, breaking off any opportunity for positive communication. Sylvia greets Raymond at the door with harsh words for being thirty minutes late from work. She doesn't ask about his day, the house is a mess, the kids are needy, and she needs help. She calls him irresponsible and says he only thinks about himself.

Raymond, on the other hand, didn't want to be late from work, but his boss kept him in a meeting that was very stressful. He then drove home in traffic and was actually looking forward to some family time. But after being greeted at the door with shame-based communication, he crawls into his cave and tries to dodge more verbal bullets.

Raymond and Sylvia go to bed exhausted and separated by a wall of deteriorating intimacy. They both love each other, but don't always like each other. As much as Sylvia hates to admit it, she is using the same communication technique that her mother used on her, a technique she always hated. And Raymond is doing what his dad always did—he closes up and quits communicating. Neither Raymond nor Sylvia is helping their relationship to achieve intimacy.

Stress Fractures

Life is difficult. A healthy marriage takes a great deal of effort and courage to achieve. No one starts out in a relationship with heightened negativity, but it seems to snowball in some relationships. The end result is an extra dose of stress, and too many couples in that situation eventually divorce. If they don't divorce they lead two parallel lives in the same house, not really connected to each other.

An unhappy marriage with lots of chronic negativity produces physical and emotional stress. As negativity seeps into the relationship, the communication looks something like a stress fracture in your foot. Let me explain. Several years ago I was preparing for a marathon. I would go out for a training run and feel a bit of pain in my foot, and when I was done running I would feel even more pain. It wasn't debilitating pain. In fact, since I had never run a marathon before, I really didn't know what "normal" training pain felt like, so I assumed I was okay. Many people from dysfunctional families don't know what normal communication feels like either.

Finally I went to a doctor, and he told me I had a stress fracture. He said the only answer was to rest the foot. If I didn't quit running, the fracture could get worse. He said, "If you just keep doing what you are doing now, I think you will be in a cast within a few weeks to a few months. A stress fracture breaks your foot very slowly, but it does cause damage." The same is true of negativity in communication. Negativity causes emotional distance, and emotional distance causes detachment. The cycle continues until the relationship is broken.

I wonder how many marriages are struggling with "stress fractures." The problem between a couple starts small, but continues to grow because of poor communication skills and an unwillingness on their part to do what it takes to repair the fracture in their relationship. For many people the answer is to go and get the help they need from a marriage expert who understands healthy communication and can help them find the patterns causing the problems in the first place. Most relationships are at least a bit high-maintenance and need constant focus and work. Sometimes we can break a bad communication habit just by being reminded that we have some things to work on. Many people have inherited their communication behavior from their parents and brought their parents' style into their own marriage.

Poor Habits of Communication

Dr. John Gottman is one of the world's leading experts on marriage. He claims that he often can determine if a couple is on the road to divorce by observing them interact on an issue of conflict. Much of his research centers around the use of negativity as poor communication. In his excellent book *The Seven Principles for Making Marriage Work*, he writes about six habits of poor communication that are detrimental to building intimacy and developing healthy communication. Looking at these can help any couple discover areas they need to work on. He calls these habits the following: (1) Harsh Start-Ups; (2) The Four Horsemen—criticism, contempt, defensiveness, stonewalling; (3) Flooding; (4) Body Language; (5) Failed Repair Attempts; (6) Bad Memories.[3]

Let me explain in my own words the dynamics behind these habits of poor communication. I think, like me, you will see yourself in many of them.

1. *Harsh Start-Ups*: This is what Sylvia did by being accusatory and negative the moment Raymond came in the door. Harsh start-ups put the other person on the defensive before the conversation has a chance to develop normally.

2. The Four Horsemen: Dr. Gottman claims that certain types of negativity are more lethal to your relationship than others. He considers these four to be particularly destructive to building intimacy:

- *Criticism.* Complaints are normal but criticism deals more with your spouse's character and personality.

- *Contempt.* This is long-simmering negative thoughts about your spouse that turn into disrespect.

- *Defensiveness.* As we discussed earlier in the chapter, this attitude rarely ever works and usually turns the conversation into a blame game.

- *Stonewalling.* Eventually your marriage partner may "tune you out." This is what is meant by stonewalling. Raymond wasn't willing to work at communication with Sylvia; he simply crawled into his cave and the conversation stopped for the time being.

3. *Flooding:* This happens when you or your spouse bombards the communication with negativity. It might take the form of criticism, contempt, defensiveness, or any other negative approach. Some people would call consistent nagging a form of flooding too. One man told me that when his wife starts flooding and nagging at him, he feels like she is taking her hand and just tapping on his chest until he blows up.

4. *Body Language:* Authorities tell us that good communication is more about body language than actual words. When a person shuts the other person out with their body language, usually the chance for healthy communication is over. Sometimes this happens because the conflict is too intense. One spouse may clearly indicate by his or her body language that he/she has quit listening. You can imagine how helpful that is for connectedness!

5. *Failed Repair Attempts:* A repair attempt is when a couple puts the brakes on the tension in the relationship and deliberately attempts to bring the intensity of the conversation down to

a more normal level. Obviously, there are times with intense communication when a couple *needs* to take a time-out. But in a relationship that isn't working, these attempts "fail"—they do not succeed at decreasing the tension or lowering the stress level. The reasons they fail are varied. Sometimes the couple is too mad or upset to make the transition. Constant failed repair attempts are like a stress fracture that just keeps getting worse.

> **When a couple is consumed with negativity it not only affects their past but it can be dangerous for their future as well.**

6. *Bad Memories:* When a couple is consumed with negativity it not only affects their past but it can be dangerous for their future as well. In almost all relationships there are very good and happy memories, but if things are too negative, the marriage partners get to the point where *they can't remember the good times*. When this happens, the relationship is deteriorating at a rapid rate.

Dr. Gottman also gives four signs that often signal that a marriage is starting to die. These are: (1) You see your marital problems as severe; (2) talking things over seems useless so you try to solve problems on your own; (3) you start leading parallel lives; and (4) loneliness sets in.[4] If your marriage is consumed with too much negativity and Dr. Gottman's four signs of a dying marriage relate to you, then I urge you to seek help. Even the most difficult of relationships can be mended if people are willing to admit need and not only seek help but then invest the energy necessary to fix the problems. Many a marriage relationship has been transformed through the power of wise counsel and good communication. Remember that sometimes before freedom comes pain, but it is worth the effort. Most likely if you are in this situation, you are feeling a bit lost and somewhat hopeless. There are answers, and there is hope for change. But you won't find it trying the same things you already have been trying. It's time to recognize your own life issues and invest in repairing your marriage.

Bill and Tanya sat with me at Starbucks after hearing me talk on negativity and marriage communication. She said, "We do all the harmful things you talked about. I love Bill, but we can't get past our poor communication to resolve our problems. We are stuck." If you feel like Bill and Tanya, you don't have to feel trapped. There is hope and healing, but you are going to have to roll up your sleeves and relearn some things about communication. You'll need to give up some habits that perhaps have been hanging around for far too long.

In fact, you may need to go back to *before* you were married and look at how your family dealt with conflict and communication. It may sound like a lot of work, but the adage from my high school basketball coach is still true: "No pain, no gain."

In the next chapter we will look at *constructive ways to improve communication* with your spouse. Now that we have examined some of the traps that inhibit intimacy and the problems that can arise from bad habits of relating, we are ready to discover the principles that can bring warmth and connectedness into any marriage situation. Healthy communication is a vital part of seeing this happen, so don't let the challenges discourage you. The results will be worth the effort—I promise!

COMMUNICATION: A KEY TO WARMTH IN YOUR MARRIAGE

QUESTIONS FOR ME

1. How would you rate your communication skills with your spouse? Poor? Okay? Good? Great? What keeps you from doing better?

2. Realizing that all marriages need work in the communication department, which point(s) in the chapter challenges you the most?

   * *over-commitment and physical exhaustion*

   * *defensiveness*

   * *addictions*

   * *negativity and shame-based communication*

   * *other:* _____

   _____

QUESTIONS FOR US

1. Describe in one or two sentences the way your family communicated when you were growing up. How has their communication or lack of communication affected the way you communicate with your spouse?

2. When you have conflict as a couple, which words describe the way you sometimes feel? Circle each word and explain why.
   Compliance
   Control

Indifference
Deadness
Feeling unloved
Distance
Fear
Growth
Love
Disapproval
Guilt
Other words:_____

HEART-TO-HEART HOMEWORK

Take some time to rank order each need, from 1 being the highest need to 10 being the lowest need, for both you and your spouse on the chart below. Then take some time to discuss your findings, feelings, and insights.

Ranking His Needs/Her Needs[5]

Mine		Spouse's
	Sexual Fulfillment	
	Recreational Companionship	
	An Attractive Spouse	
	Domestic Support	
	Admiration	
	Affection	
	Conversation	
	Honesty and Openness	
	Financial Support	
	Family Commitment	

chapter 5

Becoming a Better Communicator With Your Spouse

Does this story sound familiar?

Laura: "We just aren't close anymore. We used to talk for hours. Gary would go out of his way to do special things to let me know he was thinking about me and that he loved me. Now he comes home from work late, pets the dog, spends some time with the kids, and doesn't even bother to talk with me. He's a nice guy, but we aren't connected like we once were connected."

Gary: "We have an okay marriage, but not a great one. Laura is always so focused on the kids and the house and all her stuff that she hardly ever shows interest in me anymore. When I come home she doesn't stop what she is doing to greet me. She usually asks me to do something around the house or run an errand. My home is stressful, and my job already has me more stressed than I think it should. I just don't feel connected to Laura anymore."

Communication is at the top of the chart when it comes to developing more intimacy in your marriage. Basically, Laura and Gary have the same needs. They both need connection and emotional intimacy that comes from healthy communication. Communication is less about talking than it is about the health of the relationship. *A couple whose emotional needs are not being met rarely communicate well.* This same couple will often turn to their children, their work, or a hobby for emotional affirmation.

When the marriage relationship feels empty, it definitely affects the ability to communicate. Couples who ignore each other's emotional needs are looking for trouble. Like Gary and Laura, there is often not much malice involved; they are just not being mindful of the other's needs. When Cathy and I are feeling safe and secure with each other, we have no problem communicating and relating. But when either one of us is feeling vulnerable, that's when the negative communication dance begins.

Jesus gave a great illustration at the end of His Sermon on the Mount:

> Everyone who hears these words of mine and puts them into practice is like a wise man who built his house on the rock. The rain came down, the streams rose, and the winds blew and beat against that house; yet it did not fall, because it had its foundation on the rock. But everyone who hears these words of mine and does not put them into practice is like a foolish man who built his house on sand. The rain came down, the streams rose, and the winds blew and beat against that house, and it fell with a great crash. (Matthew 7:24–27)

ROCK-SOLID PRINCIPLES FOR GOOD COMMUNICATION

Rain, wind, and storms will come to all of our lives. If your marriage hasn't been through a storm, it will. The simple lesson of Jesus is not that storms won't come to our lives, but rather that *we must prepare for those storms.* A home and marriage built on rock-solid principles will bend and bruise, but make it through the tough times; but a home and marriage built upon "sandy principles" will probably crash. Let's look at how to build your marriage upon the rock-solid principles of healthy communication.

BE EMPATHETIC

Empathy basically means to walk in your spouse's shoes and understand life from his/her perspective. You don't even have to agree with your spouse to understand where he or she is coming from in life. Drs. Les and Leslie Parrot report, "Research has shown that 90 percent of our struggles in marriage would be resolved if we did nothing more than see that problem from our partner's perspective. Empathy is the heart loving."[1]

It took me a very long time in my marriage to understand that Cathy didn't need me to *fix* her problems. All she wanted was for me to *care*. My natural tendency is to be a fix-it person. I would get fully engaged with whatever her problem was and immediately start looking for the cure. What Cathy would rather have had was a sympathetic hug and a sense that I understood and cared about her. After I became comfortable in not always trying to be her fix-it man, I realized it was much easier on our relationship to simply let her know I value her feelings.

Dr. John Gottman says the core for good communication is "communicating basic acceptance of your partner's personality. Human nature dictates that it is virtually impossible to accept advice from someone unless you feel that that person understands you."[2] The bottom line is helping your spouse feel

> **It is virtually impossible to accept advice from someone unless you feel that that person understands you.**

like he or she is understood. Work stress, money issues, extended-family burdens, sex, housework, and parenting are all issues of marital conflict, but the most stable of marriages work at each of these issues/conflicts as *a team*. Knowing you understand and are on your spouse's side will bring safety and security to your relationship.

BE A GOOD LISTENER

Listening is the language of love. A relationship of affirmation has a lot more listening and less lecturing. I think God made two ears and one tongue for a reason. I find with Cathy that it is harder for me to suspend judgment and simply listen to her the way I would listen to a friend. Too often I want to interrupt her and try to fix her problem, or preach at her or lecture her. Yet for most of us, we don't have that same tendency when dealing with a friend. James, the Lord's brother, gave some very good advice: "Everyone should be quick to listen [and] slow to speak" (James 1:19). Pure and simple, that's good communication counsel.

I remember a time when Cathy was telling me about a problem she was having with one of our kids. I could see it was going to be a long, drawn-out conversation, and in my mind, I had a simple solution to the problem. So I kept interrupting her.

Not one to hold things back, Cathy finally blurted out, "Do you realize that interrupting me is rude? I know you wouldn't do it in a counseling session, so take a few more minutes and listen to my whole story. I want your comments . . . but not before I give you the story!" She was right. She needed me to validate her by taking the time to listen.

Usually after I watch a couple interacting with each other for only a short time I can tell what kind of a listener each person is and how they communicate. Think about when you last were with a friend who sat and really listened to you as you poured out your story. How did you feel? You probably felt loved and cared for. One of my good friends is one of the best listeners I have ever known. I am always so drawn to being with him. Because he is a good listener, the attitude that comes across to me is "I care about you." *Could your spouse say that about you?*

Effective Listening Qualities

Some couples need to stop telling each other what is wrong and just stop and listen. Listening is not always easy, especially if we think we have the right answer most of the time. Are you a good listener? Just in case you are like most of us and need to brush up on your listening skills, let me offer Seven Effective Listening Qualities.[3]

1. a genuine desire to listen to your spouse
2. a willingness to accept his/her feelings and emotions, whether he/she is right or wrong
3. a desire to not always need to be right (ouch!)
4. a nonjudgmental attitude
5. eye contact and little fidgeting
6. showing appreciation that your spouse is confiding in you
7. a willingness not only to listen, but to continue to be supportive

How did you do? If you have room for improvement, join the club. As you implement these essentials into your communication with your spouse, I believe you will see immediate gain in your relationship.

EXPRESS YOUR EXPECTATIONS

Why is it that we expect our spouse to be a mind reader? Ronnie put it this way: "My husband is so cold toward me. I love flowers, back rubs, and chocolate, and he never spontaneously gives them to me."

Now that seemed like a simple request to me. "Why do you think your husband never gives you those things?"

"I don't know. He is just so insensitive!"

"So have you told him how much you would like those gifts of flowers, chocolate, and back rubs, and he just ignores you?"

"Well, I haven't exactly *told him*. We've been married for twelve years . . . he should know my likes and dislikes."

"Now, wait a minute," I protested. "Do you expect your husband to be a mind reader?"

"He knows I like flowers and chocolate, and who doesn't like a back rub?"

"So you haven't told your husband specifically what you hope to receive from him?"

"Of course not. That would spoil the gift!"

"Okay, but you are disappointed already. I vote for *telling your husband* exactly what you want and need. I think you will be pleasantly surprised at his response." One of the biggest hurdles in most marriages is communication, but if you don't let your spouse know specifically what your expectations are, you may never get the attention you hope for in the relationship.

Later in the month I met with Ronnie and her husband. She was smiling. I asked how it was going. She said, "You tell him, honey."

Her husband looked at me a little bewildered, but he was smiling as he shook his head and reported what had happened. Apparently Ronnie came home from her conversation with me and informed him that I told her to tell him to buy her flowers and chocolates and to give her back rubs! Now, that wasn't exactly the way I remembered the conversation, but he went on to say, "I have brought flowers home for her every week. We went out for chocolate-dipped strawberries just last night in town. And I'm trying to give her a back massage most days." Ronnie then added, "It's been great!"

I think Ronnie had forgotten that during the first conversation we had she was determined not to tell her husband her needs and wants because he was just "supposed to know." Here's my advice for you regarding any marital issue, from a conflict to a desire: Don't expect your spouse to "get it." Be specific, and tell him or her exactly what you are looking for. It would be great if we all could read minds, but we can't. So we need to express our expectations clearly and simply to one another.

Resolving not to play "communication games" with each other falls under this same category. A husband recently said to me, "I don't even care if it's negative—I just want my wife to shoot straight with me." I think his desire is right on target. Good communication begins with honesty, integrity, and courage. Lies and half-truths don't produce healthy communication or true intimacy. There are no short cuts with good communication. It takes concentrated work, but it's always worth it in the long run.

If you or your spouse need help in this area, counseling is a very good option. In chapter 1, I quoted a Bible verse that speaks to this: "Where there is no counsel, the people fall; but in the multitude of counselors there is safety" (Proverbs

Good communication begins with honesty, integrity, and courage.

11:14 NKJV). There are certain problems in communication that are especially challenging for some people. Learning how to express your expectations in a positive way is one of them. If you need help in developing new habits of communication, you may find that a counselor is just what you need to progress more quickly and effectively.

Schedule Communication Times

I've been rather tough on the people who expect their spouse to spontaneously meet their needs. I'd like to continue in this same line of thinking to make another helpful suggestion. I vote for *scheduling communication* between spouses. Let me give you a very personal illustration.

For Cathy and me, dealing with the business of family life— insurance, banking, scheduling, and any other administrative task—has been a source of conflict in our marriage. You see, Cathy is a detail person, and I am not. She wants to read the fine print in the insurance papers, and I don't even know where we keep the insurance papers. It's clear that we need each other, but it can also be very frustrating to approach things in such opposite ways.

Couples tell me all the time that when it comes to taking care of life, they often see things from very different perspectives. This can be a problem if they try to take care of too many of their responsibilities on the run, without a plan. If that is your story, then you are asking for trouble. I know that not all problems are solvable. But the good news is, this one is! I can help with a workable plan for handling your business meetings, and then it's up to you to figure out who does which task.

First, *schedule your business meeting.* Don't deal with these issues every night or only whenever you have a crisis. Schedule a weekly business meeting. Cathy and I have a "not after 10:30 p.m. or before 8:00 a.m. rule" at our home. We just don't do well with a discussion on how we are going to pay our daughter's college bill at those times. Some of our harshest conversations started after 10:30 at night or before 8:00 in the morning. The harshness came primarily because we were tired and not focused on the topic. I can usually handle the logistics of family life if I am prepared emotionally for the discussion.

So set up a time and treat it like a business. Set whatever you have to deal with aside until your scheduled business meeting. If you are an agenda-type person, create an agenda. Just don't spoil other times with random family business that isn't an emergency. For Cathy and me, there are other scheduled communication times in addition to the business one. We meet weekly for a spiritual time together and we have a weekly date night. Despite what you might think, scheduled communication times actually bring freedom to our relationship, not burdens. Cathy knows she has 100 percent of my attention during a scheduled family business meeting. I will look over the insurance or anything else she needs at that time. The problems arise when she tries to discuss them when it's the ninth inning and the bases are loaded and my team is up to bat. I think you get the picture.

The point here is to *be proactive.* My friend Terry has "Sharon Days" when he gives the whole day to his wife. Sometimes they run errands, other times they go to a dinner and a play. Regardless of what they do together, he is telling her with his actions that he wants to be present in her life. Another friend has started having a once-a-month "Oasis Saturday." He and his wife take care of the kids' needs and then spend the whole day together. They take time in planning the day out so it provides them a time of fun, replenishment, and communication.

Ted and Sally take a walk most every night right after dinner. It's a chance for them to catch up with each other and lose a few calories at the same time. The regularity of this time means they can look forward to it all day. Other couples have made a habit of a regular Starbucks date or a twice-a-week breakfast appointment. Cathy and I try to plan four times a year to go away for at least a night just for communication and relationship building. As a couple, decide what your needs are and then come up with an idea that works for you.

DEVELOP A PROBLEM-SOLVING PLAN

All marriages have problems. Knowing how we solve our problems will give us a much better handle on our goal, which is to create warmth and intimacy as well as rekindle romance in our relationship. When it comes to conflict, read my lips: *Not all problems are resolvable!* I wish more marriage experts would just tell us that from the beginning. Some problems we face are perpetual. These are problems that will always be in our lives in one form or another. You will have issues in your relationship where the best you can do is agree to disagree. When that is the case, move on. Don't spend time looking for a way to resolve the problem. Rather, find a workable solution so you can both *live with it*. You do this every day at work with co-worker relationships, so make it happen with your spouse.

> You will have issues in your relationship where the best you can do is agree to disagree.

Just before writing these words, Cathy and I took our dog for a walk along a hillside that has one of our favorite views of the Pacific Ocean. It was sunset, and I had a leisurely walk in mind—a stroll to watch the sun go down over beautiful Catalina Island. Cathy, however, had not worked out yet. So in her mind we were on a *power walk*. When I stopped to admire the sunset, Cathy wanted to keep walking at a pace that was making me sweat. This is not a new problem for us! Cathy was going to have to give in to me and slow way down, or I needed to give in to her wishes and sweat.

I am happy to tell you I am finishing this section a bit sweaty because this problem wasn't the hill I was willing to defend till death. Most of our marital problems are not troubles worth putting the relationship in jeopardy over. Life isn't an emergency. The conflict doesn't usually matter as much as we make it matter. One of the helpful phrases of the late '90s was "Don't sweat the small stuff," and almost all stuff is small stuff! Another phrase to remember when we think about a problem that has no solution is what my grandpa used to say: "If the horse is dead, get off the horse."

When the problem is solvable, and you want to give it your best shot with your spouse, you might want to consider following a simple five-point process of problem-solving that has been helpful to me (explained below). Keep in mind what I once heard author and speaker Barbara Johnson say: "Never let the problem to be solved become more important than the person to be loved."

1. *Find the real problem.* Sometimes when we are communicating or in conflict with our spouse we are trying to hit a moving target. It's important to stick with one issue at a time, and make sure it is the very problem you want to solve. If you are talking just to talk, that's fine, but it isn't problem-solving. As an example, let's pretend that the problem is "We have too much debt in our lives."

2. *List alternative solutions.* Whenever possible as a couple, take a look at various solutions and try to come up with a solution that both of you can support. Remember, people support what they help create. With a problem, if *you* can become a *we*, that is a great help. Let's pretend you came up with three possible solutions:

- *Sell a car and pay off some debt.*

- *Either you or your spouse work more hours.*

* *Develop a budget with a plan to get out of debt.*

3. *Together, select a plan of action.* Now that you have looked at the alternatives and discussed each of them, come up with a plan that works for both of you. If you need to write out the plan, do that. In this case, let's pretend that you both chose the third solution: "Develop a budget with a plan to get out of debt." This means that together you create a plan that works best for you as a couple. My suggestion is that you take the extra time to write out the plan on paper so you have something concrete that both of you agreed to follow.

4. *Establish and enforce accountability.* You developed a plan. Now you need to hold each other accountable to follow the plan. With this illustration, a simple weekly report on how you spent money compared to your plan is very easy to follow. For most problem-solving, a weekly check-in time works well.

5. *Set up an evaluation procedure.* Keep it very simple, but put together some kind of an evaluation procedure to help you assess how you are doing with the problem. If you have created a budget with a plan to get out of debt, it would be as simple as creating a check and balance to make sure you are following the plan and eventually reaching your goal of being out of debt.

This is a very simple and straightforward process that takes some of the emotion out of problem-solving and helps us focus on a workable solution. Basically, what we are doing is creating a *common language* to deal with problems. If we don't create a common language to communicate, we really will feel like one of us is from Mars and the other is from Venus!

When spouses have major differences in communication style, working with each other is somewhat like learning another language. When they can find common words and phrases that make sense to both of them, all their shared activities (including problem-solving) will be more productive. They will get to their goals faster too, which means valuable time is not spent in frustration and anger with one another. Just imagine what all of this means in terms of building intimacy in our marriage relationships!

Good communication goes back to mutual respect and mutual submission. Good communication is showing respect and honor to your spouse. It is possible to bring affection, warmth, and encouragement (A.W.E.) to your marriage even in the challenging area of communication. *You can* change the tone of your relationship by changing the way you communicate with your spouse.

BECOMING A BETTER COMMUNICATOR WITH YOUR SPOUSE

QUESTIONS FOR ME

1. What can I do to be a more effective communicator with my spouse?

2. What communication skill from the list below do I most need to work on?

   * *showing empathy*

   * *being a good listener*

   * *expressing my expectations*

   * *scheduling communication times*

   * *problem-solving*

3. What would be a good first step to take in this one area?

QUESTIONS FOR US

1. In what one area of communication do we find that we are not doing as well as we once did?

2. Are there any times of communication we need to schedule in order to enhance our relationship? What would we need to deal with? What is a good day and time to do it?

HEART-TO-HEART HOMEWORK
THE PROBLEM-SOLVING PLAN

Using "The Problem-Solving Plan" in this chapter, take some time to identify a problem that you are having as a couple and try to create a workable solution for it. If you need to reread this portion of the chapter, it is found on pages 98-99. Make sure to handle only one problem at a time.

1. What is the *real* problem?

2. What are possible solutions?

3. This is the plan of action we have selected.

4. Here's how we will establish and enforce accountability.

5. Here's how and when we will evaluate how we are doing with this specific problem.

6

Encouragement:
The Friendship and
Fun Factor

Friendship and fun in a marriage are two of the biggest predictors of long-term marital satisfaction. Why is it that for many couples we move from "best friends" who have a lot of fun together before we married, to a much more intense relationship as the years go on in our marriage?

One woman said to me recently, "We have a semi-active sexual relationship but I am starved for emotional connectedness." The affection, warmth, and encouragement in a relationship do not usually have as much to do with sex as they have to do with friendship and fun. Don't get me wrong; as you read in chapter 3, sexual intimacy is very important in a relationship. However, for a relationship to sustain and thrive, it has to also have a strong dose of friendship and fun.

Authorities tell us "the determining factor in whether couples feel satisfied with the sex, romance, and passion in their marriages is, by 70 percent, the quality of the couple's friendship."[1] Authorities and common sense both tell us that the blissful state of romance just doesn't last. As time goes on, anger and resentment build up to a point where a couple can lose their closeness and friendship. Keeping the friendship factor in your marriage is one of the surest signs that you will remain connected.

Friends tend to have more patience with each other. Friends extend tons of grace and forgiveness. Friends practice kindness toward one another. Friends celebrate special occasions. Friends give each other words of affirmation. For many people, once we are married we get lazy about our friendship with our spouse. Many of the basic principles of friendship work just as well in a marriage.

Cathy and I are very different in many ways. Cathy is an introvert, and I am an extrovert. When we are at a party she will have a few meaningful conversations that go deeper, and I tend to want to meet and talk with everyone. She says my conversations are shallower, and she is probably right for the most part. We are different in many other ways, but what has kept our marriage strong is our friendship.

We both love the beach. We love to go to movies together. We walk our dog along the coast a few times a week after a regular stop at a Starbucks, where we actually get the same specialized coffee drink. When we think of the perfect vacation, it is almost always the same. We cheer for the same sports teams, we like the same food, and we enjoy the same kind of music. Before Cathy and I were married, we liked to linger with each other over a cup of coffee. Today, we still like to do the same lingering thing. I'm not sure all these things were so similar when we first started dating, but over the years our friendship has deepened, along with our love for each other. Even so, there are times when both of us need to be very proactive about working on our friendship. It takes time, energy, and focus to nurture a growing friendship. The more I talk with couples who have been married for even just a few years, the more I see this area as a problem in their relationship.

Many couples tell me that they were friends when they were dating, but now they see themselves as merely "husband and wife." Of course they *are* husband and wife, but the myth is that you cannot still be friends. Look at the couples you know who are your most inspirational examples in marriage. No doubt they are also good friends who work on that area of their relationship. The Bible says that a friend loves at all times (Proverbs 17:17) and a friend "sticks closer than a brother" (Proverbs 18:24). Friends have casual talk time. When you are married, you have to be intentional about that kind of conversation. Friends listen without blaming. Friends show respect for the other's feelings, even if they disagree. They share common passions and beliefs. Friends make each other feel safe and don't try to change each other.

Do you need to work on the friendship factor of your marriage? If you do, you definitely aren't alone. Over time, every couple's relationship can become predictable. Romance, sex, and even conversation can become routine or sometimes even nonexistent. If "routine" or "predictable" sums up your situation, then it's time to refocus some of your energy on your *friendship* with your spouse. Here are some questions to help you evaluate what needs to happen to light the spark of friendship again:

1. When you and your spouse were dating, what did you do to make him or her feel special? When was the last time you did that in your marriage?
2. What was the last fun activity that you and your spouse enjoyed together?
3. How often do you find time to just "hang out" and talk like you did before you were married?
4. If you asked your spouse to list your top five priorities (based on where you devote the most time and effort), what would those priorities be? Where does your spouse rank on the list?

ARE WE HAVING FUN YET?

Fun is a necessary ingredient to a marriage of intimacy.

Lately I have been asking people, "Do you have fun together as a couple?" The reactions are mixed, but I must tell you much of the time I get blank stares. Guys tend to joke about sexuality. Women tend to be much more honest and say something like, "I really wish we did have more fun together." Fun is a necessary ingredient to a marriage of intimacy.

A few years ago, Cathy and I were analyzing our marriage and we realized that there were some stale parts to the relationship. We talked about the amount of fun we had as a couple before we got married—the spontaneous tennis matches, hours of just talking, and late night ice cream runs. We laughed more. The responsibilities of raising three daughters, work, bills, schedules, and all the rest had drained us of our fun.

Our oldest daughter, Christy, had even remarked that someone had mentioned to her that when Cathy and I were in youth ministry *we were really fun and funny people.* She said, "I can't picture you guys being that fun or funny as youth workers. You seem too serious." Ouch! We decided right then and there that we would work on the fun factor in our lives. We wrote on the refrigerator door, "Are we having fun yet?" It was a reminder that taking the time to have fun was intentional.

Shortly after our little epiphany we decided to spontaneously take a family weekend, going away to Palm Springs to just play. Cathy and I had to reprogram ourselves because we had agendas for all three of our girls as well as work for us to complete. We purposefully left the work at home and set the agendas aside. We focused on fun. We ate fun food. We enjoyed the warmth of the sun and a pool. We rented a movie one night and ate popcorn and assorted junk food. We splurged on most everything that weekend, including our diet. The entire family looks at this as a *great weekend.* We came home to the same agendas and workload, but because we had connected as a family through fun, it made the load easier.

THE IMPORTANCE OF PLAY

In a book I wrote called *The 10 Building Blocks to a Happy Family*[2] I studied traits of healthy families and found that one of the strongest traits of healthy, happy families was *play*. This may sound like an oversimplification, but a family or a marriage that isn't "working" is a family or marriage that isn't playing. Fun builds positive memories, reduces stress, produces affirmation and support, and often causes good communication too. When you ask people about family or marriage traditions, they usually bring up fun times.

Outdoor adventure expert Tim Hansel once said, "Play is a taste of the Paradise from which we came, a foretaste of the Paradise we will enter." If you and your spouse can find time to play together, it really is a good bonding experience. Play doesn't have to be sports. Play can be a hobby. Our friends Randy and Susan took a photography class together. Terry and Sharon ski. John and Bonnie took a cooking class together, and now once a week they put together a dinner for couples from their church. It doesn't matter what you do. What matters is that as a couple (and a family), there is a fun factor in your relationship.

Cathy and I love comedy movies. We know some of the lines from movies we have seen over and over again by heart. These lines have now entered into our life. We will give one of the lines and then just start laughing. Just as I have mentioned in other chapters, we have to be *intentional* about this. You might ask, "Are you saying to schedule fun?" Sure! I don't know about scheduling laughter, but regularly putting "fun" on the calendar is a really good idea. It is therapeutic for couples to laugh together. Laughter even has health benefits.

The Bible says that "A merry heart does good, like medicine" (Proverbs 17:22 NKJV). The truth of this verse is confirmed in medical research. Laughter strengthens the immune system, burns calories, relieves stress, reduces blood pressure, reduces pain by increasing endorphins—the body's natural painkillers, improves lung capacity and oxygen levels, and provides a good massage for internal organs. And, like yawning, laughing is contagious.[3] Besides the physical health benefits, large doses of fun and laughter help to build a strong relationship with your spouse.

IDEAS TO START TODAY

I don't know about you, but when I read some of the marriage and family books in bookstores today, I tend to feel overwhelmed with all I need to do to improve. Some of it looks like just *too much work*. Working on friendship and fun in your relationship can be done with just a bit of intentional focus, and the good news is that everyone can do it. Who doesn't want more fun and friendship in life? Most conflict is rooted in unmet needs, and these are needs that often go unmet in marriage. Here are some practical ideas to address that.

Creative Dates

If you don't date much with your spouse, this is the week to plan a creative date. You don't necessarily need a lot of money, just the energy to plan something fun and enjoyable. I love to go to dinner and a movie with Cathy, but it isn't something out of the ordinary. Too many couples get in a habit of only doing the dinner and a movie date. Consider skipping rocks at the lake, feeding the ducks, flying a kite, and having a picnic . . . now that's a more creative date! It doesn't take much longer to prepare that date than going out for dinner and a movie. Your willingness to put some thought into more creative dates will speak volumes to your spouse. Just in case you need help, I will start you off with a list from my personal collection. Sometimes people will tell us that we are *so creative* with our dates. Actually, Cathy and I started with a list just like this one below and went right down the list and checked off the date as we experienced it.

1. Take a hike.
2. Hit golf balls or play miniature golf.
3. Build a snowman or a sand castle.
4. Learn to play backgammon.
5. Take a photography or dance class together.
6. Go bowling (only if it is a novelty).
7. Visit a zoo.
8. Visit a museum.
9. Attend a concert (preferably outdoors, when the weather permits).
10. Put a jigsaw puzzle together.
11. Go out for dessert first, and then have dinner.
12. Take an exercise class together.
13. Surprise your spouse with an overnight. Make all the arrangements for the baby-sitting, reservations, and whatever else is needed, and then tell your spouse.
14. Have an overnight camp-out in your backyard.
15. Go on a date in the morning. It's okay—be late for work just this one day!

Okay, I think you get the idea. These are some of our favorite dates over the years. Most didn't cost a bunch of money, but some of them did take some time to plan. For example, date #13 required Cathy working out a time to come and pick me up from work without my knowing about it. She had arranged for a special night away from our regular routine. Just five minutes from our home was a great bed-and-breakfast where we would send friends from out of town. But we had never gone there because it was so close to our house.

Working together with Cathy, my assistant created a fake appointment at 5:00 p.m. as well as a completely phony schedule for the next day. Cathy showed up at 5:00 p.m. to whisk me away. She had even packed for me. I was shocked, and I must admit it took me several minutes to move from work-responsibility mode to night-away mode. But I caught on pretty quickly. We had a wonderful twenty hours together, and I went back to work that next afternoon refreshed, grateful to Cathy, and more in love with her than ever before.

GIVE THE GIFT OF ENCOURAGEMENT AND AFFIRMATION

I'm told it takes nine affirming comments to make up for even one critical comment. If you are like most people, you owe your spouse a *boatload* of encouragement! Many people get in a very bad habit of neglecting to encourage their spouse. Sometimes we get so busy with life that we miss the major (and minor) opportunities to give our spouse the gift that keeps on giving: a genuine word of encouragement.

> **A daily dose of encouragement from you to your spouse is better than any monetary present you could give.**

Affirming words have the power to bring healing to a worn-out marriage. A daily dose of encouragement from you to your spouse is better than any monetary present you could give. Today, take the time to write a note, or better yet, look your spouse right in the eye and give him/her a compliment. You will immediately see in his/her eyes what a big deal it is to receive affirmation and encouragement. Here is your homework: Look for ways to give at least one genuine, heartfelt word of praise to your spouse every day for the next week. If you need to write down what you will say, do it. Even in the midst of tension, take the time to give a word of encouragement. You will likely see immediate appreciation and a softening that both of you will experience.

You may have heard the story about the gentleman who went to a marriage counselor to talk about divorcing his wife. The wise counselor said, "Before you do that, I want you to attempt something for me. Are you willing to try?"

The man replied, "What have I got to lose?"

"Good, then I want you to spend the next month giving encouragement and affirmation to your wife. *Treat her like a goddess.* Bring her flowers and chocolates and help her around the house. Tell her that you will do the dishes. Take her honey-do list and start working through it, beginning tonight."

The man took the advice and went straight home, where he brought his wife chocolates and flowers. He told her to sit down, and he fixed dinner. He complimented her for all her hard work and the wonderful job she had done with the kids. He took the honey-do list and got started immediately.

The next day the counselor decided to call the man to see how the first night went. He told the counselor all the wonderful things he had done for his wife. "Wow! What was her reaction?" the counselor asked.

Bill replied, "She said, 'Oh, Bill we have so many problems, and now on top of all that, you come home drunk!'"

A month later the counselor called Bill and asked if he had filed for divorce. "File for divorce? Why would I do that? I married a *goddess*!" The person who had changed was Bill because he started treating his wife with encouragement. Some people call it the self-fulfilling prophecy—you become what others believe you to be. Our job is to treat our spouse with kindness and encouragement and to constantly show affirmation. Most everyone will respond to this treatment in a positive way over time. But even if they don't because of some pathology in their life, you will be a better person for having given the gift of encouragement.

Cathy and I have had to realize that our need for encouragement from each other is huge, but our love language is very different. If Cathy writes me a card with praise in it or she tells me she appreciates me, she has given me all I need to go on for weeks because I appreciate so much her words of affirmation.

I expected that to be true for Cathy as well. So I would write her notes and whisper words of encouragement. I could see that she always appreciated affirmation, but she responded most positively when I "encouraged" her by folding the laundry or doing the vacuuming. Basically, Cathy would rather have me help with the dishes than send her a love note while she is washing the dishes alone! Maybe it's time to find out your spouse's love language—the ways your spouse likes to be encouraged. The best way to do that is to ask. But then, you probably already know the answer.

FLIRT!

Just because you are married doesn't mean you can't flirt— with each other. Flirting is a flattering way to remind your spouse of your constant affection. Flirting is not appropriate with others, but it tells your spouse you are thinking about him/her. I love these ideas from Doug Fields' book *100 Fun and Fabulous Ways to Flirt With Your Spouse*[4].

1. Write a love story about how you met and get it printed and bound.
2. Whisper something romantic to your spouse in a crowded room. (One of my favorites!)
3. Mail a love letter to your spouse at work.
4. Put on your spouse's favorite romantic music and take her dancing around your candlelit living room.
5. Remember to look in your spouse's eyes when he/she tells you about his/her day.
6. Snuggle together on the sofa and reminisce through old photo albums.

The Power of Touch

Physical touch is very important in building an intimate relationship. Many women tell me that they wish they could just cuddle with their spouse and it would not *always* lead to sex. Part of flirting is just snuggling with your spouse. One woman said that she and her husband start the morning waking up to the alarm, but stay in bed snuggling for the next ten minutes until the snooze alarm goes off again. They then pray for their day and get up to make the most of their next several hours. No wonder they have a healthy relationship!

Physical touch is obviously more than flirting, but it is important in building romance and intimacy. I don't just mean foreplay, but a touch that says, "I appreciate you." Coming up from behind and giving your spouse a neck massage, for example, says, "I am thinking about you, and I love you."

Dr. Louis McBurney and his wife, Melissa, have helped thousands of couples reconnect in their marriages. His own story about the power of touch goes like this:

> Any friendship is built on reciprocal giving to meet the other person's needs. It's the spiritual principle of reaping what you sow and it works in marriage as well as in other relationships. Because of our desire to meet one another's needs, I fill Melissa's emotional bank account through "non-sexual" touch and she responds with red-hot lovin'. Works well for us![5]

"Any friendship is built on reciprocal giving to meet the other person's needs."

If you put into practice the art of encouraging your spouse through deepening your friendship and enjoying fun times, you won't have to wind up like a couple I read about on the Internet:

> A woman accompanied her husband to the doctor's office. After his checkup, the doctor called the wife into his office alone. He said, "Your husband is suffering from a very severe disease, combined with horrible stress. If you don't do the following, your husband will surely die: Each morning fix him a healthy breakfast. Be pleasant and make sure he is in a good mood. For lunch make him a nutritious meal. For dinner prepare an especially nice meal for him. Don't burden him with chores, as he's probably had a hard day. Don't discuss your problems with him; it will only make his stress worse. And, most important, satisfy his every whim. If you can do this for the next ten months to a year, I think your husband will regain his health completely."
>
> On the way home, the husband asked his wife, "What did the doctor say?"
>
> "You're going to die," she replied.

Obviously, it's a corny joke. But a relationship with a solid friendship, lots of fun, some flirting going on regularly, and physical touch is a very encouraging and healthy relationship.

ENCOURAGEMENT: THE FRIENDSHIP AND FUN FACTOR

QUESTIONS FOR ME

1. What can I do to be a better friend to my spouse? What can I do to bring more fun to our marriage?

2. How would my bringing friendship and fun to my marriage be an encouragement to my spouse?

QUESTIONS FOR US

1. Reminisce about your top ten fun experiences as a couple. List them below.

    1.

    2.

    3.

    4.

    5.

    6.

    7.

    8.

    9.

    10.

2. If it has been a while since you had fun as a couple, what could you do to improve the fun factor?

3. When in your relationship did you feel like "best friends"? How would you say it is going today?

HEART-TO-HEART HOMEWORK
CREATIVE DATES

Brainstorm twenty creative date ideas and then attempt to do all twenty of them within the year.

1.
2.
3.
4.
5.
6.
7.
8.
9.
10.
11.
12.
13.
14.
15.
16.
17.
18.
19.
20.

chapter 7

Finding Intimacy and Freedom Through Forgiveness

God's forgiveness is staggering. I am constantly amazed at the number of Bible verses that touch on grace and forgiveness. Forgiveness goes against our human nature, but it is an essential characteristic of our loving God. And His desire is to impart this to us as well. Since God's forgiveness is so strong and powerful, we see how forgiveness can transform our human relationships as well, releasing them from a prison of resentment, bitterness, and anger. There is no doubt about it: Without forgiveness in a marriage, the relationship will flounder. But with forgiveness, we can find intimacy and freedom even in the midst of our brokenness. Some of the finest marriages I know have experienced the lowest of lows and climbed back to A.W.E. because of the power of forgiveness.

Research shows that many marriages are destroyed by the resentment that builds up when couples hurt each other. The problem is, *all* couples hurt each other in one way or another.

Some couples are able to get beyond the pain from put-downs, affairs, forgetfulness, bad decisions, negative interpretations, abusive comments, rudeness, thoughtlessness, as well as a hundred other harmful things, and still find happiness on the other side. How is it possible? I think it is because those couples have learned how to forgive.

Every couple has a need for forgiveness, because all spouses are dysfunctional in one way or another. The words we have said, the things we have done, and the brokenness and sinfulness in our own lives are often harshest toward our spouse. When you think about the many offenses we have done to each other, it is a wonder there aren't *more* divorces than the 50 percent statistic we see in the news.

Your story may be different from your neighbor's, but one thing is certain: You have offended your spouse because of wrongdoing and you need to ask for forgiveness. Jeff had an affair. Connie is addicted to prescription drugs. When Carol feels stress, which is most of the time, this sweet churchgoing saint cusses out her husband like a sailor. Hurtful words, wrong actions, lying, cheating, gossip, sexual impropriety—all are ways of describing your sinful nature. In the midst of all of this, God loves you and forgives you. Your response to this kind of forgiveness should be to do the same for your spouse. This doesn't mean your spouse should not take responsibility for his/her actions. What it does mean is that we have work to do in our own lives *before* we focus on our spouse. They deserve from us the same kind of forgiveness God gives to us.

I love this story of Corrie ten Boom, who spent several years in a German concentration camp in some of the worst conditions I've ever heard about in human history. If she could learn the lesson of forgiveness and discover the freedom it brings, then there is hope for any marriage. The year was 1947. It was almost two full years after the liberation of Auschwitz, the camp where she and her sister had been kept captive by the Germans. Corrie was in a Lutheran church to share her story. As she stepped forward she prayed that God would use her words to bring about healing, forgiveness, and restoration in the lives of those who heard her. But what she was about to experience would change *her* life forever.

When she finished her message a man stepped forward, moving his way through the crowd of people waiting to talk to Corrie. He looked familiar, like she'd seen him somewhere before. As she looked into his eyes, it all became crystal clear. She recognized him . . . the uniform . . . the whips . . . walking past him naked at the selection. She remembered her sister dying a slow and painful death at his hands. The memories came flooding back to her . . . memories from Auschwitz and this man who had been a guard at the camp.

"I'm a Christian now." He spoke with his eyes looking sadly into hers. "I know that God has forgiven me, but will *you* forgive me?" He stretched out his hand to receive hers.

She stood there for what must have seemed an eternity, although it was probably only a moment or two. She knew that she needed to make a choice. Would she forgive the man at whose hand she had experienced so much hurt, pain, and humiliation? Would she? Could she?

Silently she prayed, "Jesus, I need your help. I can lift my hand, but you need to supply the feeling." She slowly raised her hand, reached out to the man, and took his hand in hers. As she did so a warm sensation filled her heart. God was indeed faithful. "I forgive you, brother—with my whole heart!"[1]

That day, former guard and former prisoner were both healed and set free from the bondage of bitterness and anger. Obviously, this is not a story about a marriage relationship (and the guard never became Corrie's best friend), but the same lesson she learned is what marriages need today as well: When we act in obedience to extend forgiveness to someone who does not deserve it, God will supply the grace for us to be able to follow through. As in Corrie's case, we sometimes even experience the warm feelings that confirm how right the decision was.

It is not always easy to extend forgiveness, but it does bring tremendous rewards. Is there a block in your relationship with your spouse that keeps you from freedom, healing, and ultimately intimacy? If so, I hope you will press on. Learning to forgive may do more for you and your marriage than any other part of this book.

Here is what the Bible says: "Be kind and compassionate to one another, forgiving each other, just as in Christ God forgave you" (Ephesians 4:32). Just about the time I want to hold something against Cathy, I read that verse and am reminded that whatever she has done to me is not as bad as what I have done to God. Yet God through Christ has forgiven me.

It is hypocritical for me to hold something against Cathy and at the same time be grateful to God for forgiving me for my sins. As I already mentioned, this thought goes absolutely against our human nature, but we can't deny its truth or its power to change our hearts. Forgiving others for their offenses against us doesn't mean we should just bury the offense or refuse to deal with the issues raised by the sin. If we do that, the offense will come back to haunt our relationship. What it does mean is that we face issues and deal with them through healthy communication, and then find the strength to forgive. The following thoughts may help.

GOD'S FORGIVENESS IS STAGGERING

Not everyone reading this book is a Christian, and by no means is this meant to be a theological work. There are far better people to write on the subject. However, the biblical teaching on forgiveness is very helpful when we attempt to forgive our spouse, as well as others. God's ways are different than our ways. While He loves unconditionally and sacrificially, we tend to hold grudges and make our love conditional. The word *gospel* literally means *good news*. Yet many Christians and non-Christians alike have a hard time fully comprehending God's love and the unmerited favor He gives to us. Look at these words from the Bible:

As high as heaven is over the earth, so strong is his love to those who fear him. And as far as the sunrise is from sunset, he has separated us from our sins. (Psalm 103:11–12 THE MESSAGE)

No matter how deep the stain of your sins, I can remove it. I can make you as clean as freshly fallen snow. Even if you are stained as red as crimson, I can make you as white as wool. (Isaiah 1:18 NLT)

But if we confess our sins to him, he is faithful and just to forgive us and to cleanse us from every wrong. (1 John 1:9 NLT)

These words from the Bible are just about the opposite of how we have been treated by others and how we at times have treated our spouse. God's grace and forgiveness are radically different from the world's standards.

A man and woman came up to me after I had just finished speaking on this topic. They poured out their story, and it wasn't pretty. Both had addiction issues and both had deeply betrayed each other. It was obvious that only God's intervention and an imparting of His healing forgiveness could change their hearts. The man was sorrowful for his horrible actions toward his wife. He asked me a question that stopped me in my tracks: "I have done so many things wrong in my life and experienced countless betrayals toward my wife. I have come to God before and with my whole heart asked for His grace and mercy. Can I really come to God *again* after failing Him and everybody else so many times? I don't deserve His forgiveness."

At that moment I remembered something Max Lucado had said about a similar situation and I paraphrased him in my response to this man. "Pardon my bluntness, but you didn't deserve forgiveness the first time you came to Christ. He knew your every sin and thought, past and present, and He forgave you anyway."

Before you work on forgiving your spouse, you must know why you were forgiven. You were not forgiven because of what you did, but because of what *Christ did*. You are not special because of what you do, but because of who you belong to; you are a child of God. Forgiveness brings healing. First the healing comes to you, and then you can offer it to your spouse. Max Lucado explained this so well: "Because you have been forgiven, forget taking shortcuts, stay on the road. He knows the way. He drew the map. He'll take you toward health and healing."[2] As you work on this important concept, live like you are forgiven. *Be healed by God's staggering words of acceptance and love.*

Before you work on forgiving your spouse, you must know why you were forgiven.

GET OUT OF THE JUDGMENT BUSINESS

Nowhere in the Bible does it say to confess your spouse's sins or your children's sins. It says, "Confess *your* sins" (James 5:16). In fact, Jesus said, "Why worry about a speck in your friend's eye when you have a log in your own?" (Matthew 7:3 NLT). He was rather clear about that issue, wasn't He? People who are judgmental, critical, and constantly negative are unhappy people. Have you ever met a judgmental person who was happy and positive about life? It is very hard not to be judgmental toward our spouses, because we know their faults and sins so well. Yet again, Jesus did not mince words: "Stop judging others, and you will not be judged. . . . Whatever measure you use in judging others, it will be used to measure how you are judged" (Matthew 7:1–2 NLT).

Life-Changing Decisions

Natalie was a very bitter woman. She had her own problems with alcoholism, but her husband had betrayed her with numerous affairs early in their marriage. Finally after twenty years of marriage, he confessed his infidelity that had taken place during their first five years together. He was wrong. She had every right to be angry. She had been betrayed and lied to over and over again. In her anger she continued to medicate her pain with alcohol. She then asked for a divorce. She spent most of her waking moments harboring venomous hatred toward her former husband and as a result became a bitter, judgmental woman.

After the divorce was final, her husband pulled his life together. He was involved in a small accountability group with other men in his church and ended up going into full-time ministry. He was a broken man with a wounded heart, but somehow he was able to accept the forgiveness of God. He told Natalie that he deserved her anger and sought her forgiveness for what he had done.

She remained angry. She was angry that the kids liked their dad more than her. She was angry that the church had restored her husband, even allowing him to work in full-time ministry. She was angry with the counselors and pastors who came alongside her husband during his healing process. I had been one of those people, and I knew her husband well. He was devastated from his past, but by receiving the forgiveness of God he was able to move on. Sure there is a hole in his heart from his past actions, but they were committed more than fifteen years ago. He could either wallow in his sinfulness or accept the staggering forgiveness of God. He chose the good news. His ex-wife chose the path of bitterness and pain.

Because we live in the same neighborhood, I ran into Natalie at the mall one day. I went over to greet her. Knowing I had been spending time with her ex-husband, she started our conversation by giving me a litany of his past sins. I said, "I am so sorry you had to go through so much." Then she turned on me and said, "How can you even stand to be in his presence?"

I replied, "Natalie, he reached out for help, so I have stood by him. I don't condone his infidelity toward you. I grieve for anyone who has been betrayed. But he is getting better and healthier. I'm afraid this has caused you, on the other hand, to become so angry and bitter that you are miserable." I went on to say, "I hope you find it in your heart to seek help for your own healing. And again, I truly am sorry for your pain."

She looked at me with burning eyes, and said, "Go to hell, Jim Burns!" Then she walked away. I wrote her a note and tried to mend the broken relationship, but she chose to be the one who *would not* forgive. In that one act, even though she was not the one to blame for the betrayal, she resigned herself to a life of misery.

Your first step toward your own healing is to *get out of the judging business*. The principle before us goes like this: The other person may be as wrong as wrong can be, but I'll not be the judge of them. I'll leave that to God. The key to forgiving others is to quit focusing on what they did and focus on what God has done for you.

FORGIVE YOUR SPOUSE AND FIND FREEDOM

> **Unforgiving people always end up in prison—a prison of anger.**

If your marriage relationship is broken, you can't possibly be healed of your emotional and spiritual hurt until you forgive your spouse. As shown in the illustration about Natalie, unforgiving people always end up in prison—a prison of anger, broken relationships, blocked faith, guilt, and personal brokenness. In these cases God doesn't have to put us in jail. We create our own prison.

If you are carrying a load of bitterness and resentment that is heavy to bear, do yourself a favor. Forgive, and be set free. Corrie ten Boom put her hand out to the guard and she was freed. Natalie, on the other hand, chose to bear the physical, mental, emotional, and spiritual burden of resentment and she remains in a prison of rage. The mountain of life issues in any relationship is too steep for anyone to continue to carry. Let the heaviness of anger and resentment go. Forgive as God forgave you. I guarantee you will not be called upon to give any more grace than God has given you.

Before we move on, I do need to mention that it is possible in relationships to forgive and not necessarily reconcile with the offending person. If you are in an abusive relationship or one filled with affairs or addictions, then you will want to get the wisdom and counsel of a trusted counselor to help you work through your own brokenness caused partly from the traumatic relationship you have been in. You don't want to adopt a Pollyanna approach, forgiving and then moving back into an abusive relationship. There are consequences to sin and brokenness, and sometimes that means you have to do your part to create healthy boundaries. Get the help you need from someone who can understand your situation and your patterns. Don't move back into a relationship where you are in danger.

Keep in mind that forgiving someone does not mean you won't feel any more pain over the incident. Also, when you forgive it doesn't mean that the person who has hurt you shouldn't take responsibility for his or her action. It isn't your job to judge them, but it doesn't mean you have to be friends with the people you forgive either.

How to Forgive Your Spouse

Every time you are on an airplane, the flight attendant comes on the intercom and says, "In case of an emergency, first put on your oxygen mask, and then help the person next to you." The reason is obvious. If you don't have adequate oxygen yourself, you won't be able to help anyone else. In the same way, the process of forgiving your spouse focuses first on you, and then extends to your spouse.

A wonderful mentor in my life years ago taught me a simple method for applying forgiveness, and it has been invaluable in my own marriage. Even if the issue that needs forgiveness in your marriage is usually more about your spouse than it is about you, there are six questions to ask yourself that are helpful. They can bring great understanding and the freedom to either forgive or be forgiven. This process is meant to be done alone, before you would ever talk with your spouse about the incident.

The Process of Forgiveness Sheet

1. What happened?
   What was the offense that continues to bother you? Be specific and give as much detail as you can. (I actually write it out in my journal.)
2. How did I feel?
   What were my emotions: Disappointment? Hurt? Do I feel angry or resentful? Did it cause me to be lonely or depressed?
3. How did I react?
   Did I get angry? Pout? Refuse to talk about it? Pull inward?

These first three questions help me get in touch with my feelings, emotions, concerns, and reactions. They also help me to focus on what exactly it is that is causing my hurt. The next three questions move toward reconciliation, but again I am looking at *my* issues, not Cathy's. These three questions involve some very spiritual-sounding words: *confession, forgiveness, repentance.* They will bring us toward reconciliation and forgiveness.

1. *Confession:* What was my part in the conflict?
2. *Forgiveness:* What do I need to forgive my spouse for and is there something I need to ask forgiveness for in this conflict? I need to ask forgiveness for _____. I forgive my spouse for _____. (Remember, I can still feel pain and hurt. Yet in faith, I choose to forgive my spouse. Often the positive feelings will come later.)
3. *Repentance:* What will I do about it?

Let me give you a personal illustration of how this worked for Cathy and me. In a conflict that I was having with her, I found myself being very upset with Cathy, because I felt like she was not paying enough attention to me. She was busy with the kids and her church activities, and in addition she had volunteered to co-chair the Grad Night committee at my daughter's high school. (This task was more than a full-time job, and the list kept going with her various involvements.) I didn't think she was being malicious. In my mind, she was just preoccupied with spinning too many plates in her life and, in my humble opinion, not paying enough attention to poor me. So I filled out the Process of Forgiveness Sheet, not really knowing what to expect.

1. What happened? *Cathy is so busy with everything else that she is not spending quality time with me.*

2. How do I feel? *I feel hurt and lonely. I feel isolated, like I'm not very important in her life.*

3. How did I react? *At first I pouted and crawled into my own cave. I spent more time at work. Then I dropped subtle and not-so-subtle hints through sarcasm that she didn't pick up on. She basically ignored my hints.*

Now I needed to focus on *my issues.* I really didn't know what would come out as I did this sheet.

1. *Confession.* What was my part in the conflict?

> **I was resenting something in our relationship that in essence I had created!**

As I stared at the sheet, I realized that during the first ten years of our marriage I had not really given the right priority to Cathy and our relationship. As discussed in chapter 2, I had often put my job ahead of our relationship. I was gone a great deal of the time. The result was that Cathy had learned to develop outside interests to work around my not always "being there" for her. I was resenting something in our relationship that in essence I had created!

2. *Forgiveness.* What do I need to forgive Cathy for and what do I need to ask for forgiveness for?

I needed to forgive Cathy for not paying enough attention to me. (But now this was not as major an issue as it was before because I needed to go back to those first ten years and ask for her forgiveness for my self-centered actions). I need to say to her, "As we have talked about in the past, I did not give you the proper attention and focus during the first ten years of our marriage. Too often I put my work and sometimes other relationships ahead of you. I am truly sorry and I ask for your forgiveness."

3. *Repentance.* What will I do about it?

I needed to tell her my concern about feeling a bit isolated from her and reassure her that I want to be more involved in her life. Actions speak louder than words, so I need to *act upon* my desire to build a more intimate relationship.

Here's what happened. I worked the sheet and then asked her out to dinner. I told her I had something I wanted to talk about. She immediately started asking about health issues and other things spouses are supposed to worry about! I reassured her it was none of that. I told her I needed about five minutes to get the whole story out before we had dialogue. (In the past, when we had conversations about issues of concern, we ended up getting defensive before the entire story was told and we often missed the point.)

Over a plate of pasta, I told Cathy what was happening in my head. I shared my feelings and how I had been reacting to them by pulling back and feeling resentment. However, I quickly added that after thinking about it, I had a revelation about our relationship and now I could see that the issue was more about me than about her. I asked for her forgiveness for how I had put work ahead of her at times—especially during the first ten years of our marriage. I said, "I ask for your forgiveness."

She said, "Jim, we have covered that, and it really is not an issue in my life anymore. I trust you, and I have seen the changes you have made." I was thinking we might be gearing up for a conflict, but she went on to ask: "So you think I have been ignoring you?"

I said, "Well, yes, I do think that at times—especially in this busy season that has taken so much of your time." Her suggestion was for us to take a weekend away and just focus on each other. She made changes, and I made changes. The process worked! (Incidentally, because I told her we weren't spending enough time together, she made me her assistant as the co-chair of the Grad Night committee so "we could spend more time together." I was such an easy target!)

Forgiveness is a key that unlocks a blocked relationship. It is possible to forgive without God's help, but my suggestion is to make your process of forgiveness a part of your spiritual discipline. With God's help you will find it easier to do than when you try to do it on your own.

You can be bitter or better. I hope you choose the freedom to forgive. I still remember the history lesson from high school about Clara Barton, the founder of the Red Cross. When one of her colleagues asked her about a situation where she could have had a great deal of bitterness, she replied: "I distinctly remember that I chose to forget that offense and move on with life." Still good thoughts from Clara after all these years!

Is there something you are holding on to with your spouse? Do you have a difficult time choosing to forgive and move on? If you struggle, you are normal. However, the most courageous marriages find intimacy and freedom through forgiveness. Yes, you have to face the issues. You can't bury or repress the problems. It's complicated, and no one said it would be easy. But choosing forgiveness for you and for your spouse is one of the healthiest decisions you can ever make. The choice is yours; the help comes from God.

FINDING INTIMACY AND FREEDOM THROUGH FORGIVENESS

QUESTIONS FOR ME

1. When have you experienced the power of forgiveness in your own life?

2. Is there something you need to forgive your spouse for in your relationship? If so, what is holding you back?

QUESTIONS FOR US

1. What is the single most powerful act of forgiveness your spouse has given to you that has brought you closer to each other?

2. Are there areas of your relationship where you have been judgmental with each other?

3. This chapter was filled with thoughts on the staggering forgiveness of God. Has there been a time in your life when you experienced the freedom of His forgiveness? Share these thoughts with your spouse.

HEART-TO-HEART HOMEWORK
THE PROCESS OF FORGIVENESS SHEET

The Process of Forgiveness was introduced to you in this chapter. If you need to review the plan you can read about it on pages 126-127. After both of you work on your own Process of

Forgiveness Sheet, share your answers with your spouse.
1. What happened?

What was the offense that still bothers you? Be specific and give as much detail as you can.

2. How did I feel?

What were my emotions: Disappointment? Hurt? Do I feel angry or resentful? Did it cause me to be lonely or depressed?

3. How did I react?

Did I get angry? Pout? Refuse to talk about it? Pull inward?

1. *Confession:*
What was my part in the conflict?

2. *Forgiveness:*
What do I need to forgive my spouse for, and is there something I need to ask forgiveness for in this conflict? I need to ask forgiveness for _____.
I forgive my spouse for _____.

3. *Repentance:*
What will I do about it?

chapter 8

Attitude Is Everything

The circumstances in your marriage may never change, but your attitude *can change* and that makes all the difference in the world! If you want to create an atmosphere of A.W.E. for your home and marriage, then you'll want to focus on your attitude first. We have already discussed that your marriage can change for the better in a matter of days with the right attitude being demonstrated by even one spouse.

At a recent conference where I was speaking, Jennifer came up to me and told me that she had been practicing A.W.E. in her marriage for the past year with great results. What had been a dull, dutiful, negative relationship was now more exciting than even the first days of their marriage.

I asked, "What happened?" and she explained it as follows.

I made a decision to change my attitude. My husband is a good guy, working hard to support the family. He would come home upbeat from work, and the moment he stepped in the door, I would begin to nag, control, and complain about life. I would watch his demeanor move quickly from "glad to see you" to "get me out of here."

One day after hearing about A.W.E., I decided to try an

experiment. I committed to a *no complaint week*. The very next day, I cleaned myself up before he came home, put on a cute outfit, and greeted him at the door by wrapping my arms around him and laying a big passionate kiss on him. He gave me kind of a weird look and then took me in his arms and kissed me again. I think he was waiting for the daily barrage of complaints . . . and they never came. Immediately he was engaged with me and the kids, and even that night was a special time of romance.

I had been stuck in a pattern of complaining, not realizing that there were other ways of handling life. The next day at work I emailed him a message, saying, "Thanks for a great evening. I love you and I'm proud to be your wife." After a week of not complaining went by, I could see how the nagging and critical spirit that I had developed over the years had created a tense living situation for all of us. I'm so glad that I can decide to change that—to create an atmosphere of A.W.E. in our home. When I do, everyone wins!

Jennifer made a courageous decision to change her attitude, and so can you. Abraham Lincoln said it best: "People are just about as happy as they make up their minds to be." If you are miserable in your marriage, or any other aspect of your life, you may be able to point to a series of circumstances that you might say caused your misery. At the risk of sounding brash or trite, let me say that your circumstances didn't make you as miserable as you might think. It was more your attitude—how you chose to *respond* to your circumstances—that determined how unhappy you were. Let the following illustration speak to your heart.

An elderly blind woman was being moved to a nursing home. When she arrived she was taken to her room, and upon entering she told her attendant enthusiastically, "I love it!"

The attendant was puzzled by this and asked the woman, "How can you say you *love it* when you've never seen it before?"

She explained: "Seeing the room doesn't have anything to do with it. Happiness is *my choice*. Every morning I have a choice, whether I'll focus on what I don't like about my life or what I do like about it. I'm choosing right now *to love* my new room where I'm going to live."

Life has its share of trials. Everyone will face situations that are less than desirable: health issues, financial loss, relationship burdens, death, not to mention life's little everyday stressors. I would never minimize those challenges. Yet so much about the quality of our lives is determined not by the situation itself, but by how we respond to it. Choosing joy for our life and our marriage is always a better option than choosing bitterness or despair.

You have a choice to make about your marriage. You can either create an atmosphere of A. W.E. regardless of how your spouse acts, or you can take your marriage to a more destructive place with negativity and complaining. An environment of negativity and tension is hard on everyone, but some people are too lazy or stubborn to make the decision to change their attitude. Don't let that be you! When you change your attitude, you'll change your marriage. Here are five practical ways to adjust your attitude to make your marriage stronger and more loving.

When you change your attitude, you'll change your marriage.

FIVE IMPORTANT ATTITUDE ADJUSTMENTS

1. STOP COMPLAINING!

"Do all things without complaining and disputing" (Philippians 2:14 NKJV).

First and foremost, you have to acknowledge that complaining is not a positive action, and it doesn't motivate anyone to change. In fact, it's been proven that just the opposite takes place; *constant criticism shuts down intimacy.* Stop hounding your spouse to death while at the same time telling her you love her unconditionally. The mixed message is too confusing, and your spouse will quite naturally react to the negative rather than the positive.

Try to remember back to a time when your parents or someone else was constantly critical of you. Did it produce warm feelings? Of course not. Constant criticism destroys warm feelings and makes both you and your spouse feel less in love with each other. When a person is controlling or negative it forces the other person to pull away.

One day I came home from work exhausted and feeling less than positive about life. Cathy asked me a question regarding a simple chore I had said I would complete that day. I hadn't even thought about it. My emotional and physical bank account must have been quite low because I was immediately defensive and lashed out at her. It was totally uncalled for and I knew it, but for some reason it made me feel good to be whiney and negative. All of a sudden the phone rang, and immediately I turned into "Mr. Nice Guy" with a salesperson.

When I hung up Cathy looked at me with hurt in her eyes and remarked, "Interesting that you could be so nice and totally present for a salesperson after you came home and started being so grumpy with me. I'm sorry you had a bad day, but don't bring your bad day into this kitchen." Ouch! Though her comment really stung, it reminded me that an attitude of A.W.E. would have been a much more effective way to handle my relationship with Cathy. It wasn't her fault I had a bad day. If I had enough reserves to be positive for the salesperson who called, I could have mustered up enough for her too.

Most people who complain that they are not getting what they want from their spouse should stop and look at how often they are disrespectful and disdainful toward him or her. The vast majority of the people who complain about their spouses often work harder to impress a stranger than to impress the one who is supposed to be the most important person in their life. Personal change is difficult, while complaining about someone else is easy. If you want to see an immediate difference in your marriage, then you will need to quit complaining and show some gratitude.

2. SHOW GRATITUDE

"Give thanks in all circumstances, for this is God's will for you in Christ Jesus" (1 Thessalonians 5:18).

An attitude of gratitude transcends circumstances. What drew you toward your spouse? What are the traits that you appreciate about her/him? Have you told your spouse lately how much you appreciate him or her? Happily married couples aren't happy because of their bank account, physique, or the fact that they never have arguments. What they do have is an attitude of gratefulness for their spouse.

One of the ways this has worked for me is by practicing what I call "thank therapy." I list at least twenty reasons why I am thankful that Cathy is my wife. Sure, there are days and even seasons when our partnership is dry or we don't seem to be running our marriage on all cylinders. But that is exactly when we *need* to practice thank therapy.

With three daughters in the home there are days when there is an extra amount of hormones and drama in the Burns household. On one such day, I came home to find the three girls and Cathy caught up in an emotional whirlwind. Cathy snapped at me, and I immediately did what many men do—I withdrew and, figuratively speaking, crawled into my cave. I was frustrated, and the last thing I wanted to do was get near the center of the storm.

After a while I felt a gentle tug on my heart from God, and I heard this still, small voice inside my head say, "Practice what you've been preaching. Practice thank therapy." So I did. With gritted teeth I growled, "Thank you, Lord, for all these hormones! Thanks for the drama. Thank you for Cathy and Christy, Rebecca and Heidi." It then dawned on me to think about the many sacrifices Cathy had made for our relationship and the ministry. I relaxed my jaw as I continued, "Thank you so much for Cathy's servant heart; she so often places the children's needs before her own. Thank you for her beauty inside and out. Thank you for her giving spirit. Thank you for her heart for the poor and oppressed. Thank you for all she does for so many people. Thank you that she puts up with me! Thank you . . . Thank you . . . Thank you . . ."

I ended up forgetting what it was exactly that sent me into my cave! I went into the living room where Cathy was folding clothes, talking on the phone to a hurting friend, and helping Heidi with her homework. I planted a kiss on her lips in the middle of her conversation and said, "I love you and thank you for being you." My circumstance hadn't changed, but with a grateful heart *my attitude had changed.* I could have stayed mad and frustrated, of course, but what good would it have done?

Our friend Terri told me she had been extra cantankerous with her husband recently. She said she had moved back toward being her old self, which in her words could be controlling, negative, nagging, and complaining. She knew her husband, Bart, had been resenting her and was becoming an expert at being a cave dweller.

Instead of demanding that he come out of the cave, she tried another tactic. First, she made sure that the kids were well fed before going to stay at a friend's house. Once they were gone, she quickly hung up a banner near the dinner table that read: *Bart, thank you for being a great: husband, dad, provider, and Christian role model. I love you more today than ever before. I am the luckiest girl in the world! Love forever, Terri.* Then she called Bart to make sure he would be home on time. She prepared his favorite meal and served it by candlelight in an outfit that, shall we say, she wouldn't wear if the kids were around. I'm sure I don't need to tell you what Bart's response was to all this attention! Basically, when you show gratitude, respect, appreciation, and some good romance, your spouse will be yours forever.

Authorities tell us that it takes just three weeks to form a habit and another three weeks to solidify that habit for a lifetime.

If you have developed a habit of being negative for most of your marriage it may take longer than three weeks. But I guarantee that if you start practicing thank therapy with gratitude, and you erase some of your negativity, your life will improve. Make gratitude a daily habit.

3. PRACTICE THE GOLDEN RULE

"In everything, do to others what you would have them do to you" (Matthew 7:12).

If your spouse feels appreciated, honored, respected, and loved, those feelings will most likely be reciprocated. The Golden Rule instructs us to treat others how we want to be treated, and eventually they will show the same respect to us. But here is the secret behind practicing this principle. Show appreciation, honor, respect, and love to your spouse even if he or she doesn't immediately reciprocate that kindness. You will be a better person for it.

At a marriage conference I was leading, Barbara shared with me a conversation she'd had with her husband. On the first night of the retreat, he said that at work he felt affirmed and successful and he spent his day with pleasant people. But at home he felt judged and condemned by his unhappy wife. He admitted to her that he spent more time at work because he felt so unappreciated and undervalued at home. That night they had a fight and went to bed without resolving it.

After Barbara finished sharing this with me, I asked her a simple question: "How would you want to be treated when you came home from work?" She immediately became defensive and started telling me all her problems. Then she stopped mid-sentence. It was as if a light bulb went on in her head. She looked at me and said, "You're right. I should think about the way I would want to be treated when I come home from work. I have done a really poor job at making my husband feel special." She gave me a hug and went to find her husband. What I laughed about after she left was that she said I was "right." I hadn't even given her a suggestion! All I did was ask a simple question, "How would *you want to be treated* when you came home from work?"

The Golden Rule is a very powerful principle for couples as long as they don't expect anything to be reciprocated immediately. When you shower your spouse with unsolicited and extraordinary love and support, your relationship will be strengthened—but it may take a while. One evening at a conference I suggested to a complaining husband that he practice the Golden Rule with his wife.

He said, "If I do that, how can I be assured that she will change?" My comment to him was, "You can't. There is no assurance that your good behavior will be rewarded. If your only reason for practicing the Golden Rule is to gain a certain response from your wife, then it won't work anyway."

4. CONTROL THE "IF ONLY'S"

"Let your 'Yes' be yes, and your 'No,' no" (James 5:12).

A marriage based on "if only's" is never very healthy. If you find yourself thinking, *If only my spouse would lose weight . . . If only my spouse would work less . . .*

Don't expect the other person to be your solution.

If only my spouse would be more romantic . . . and so on, you are setting yourself up for disappointment. This kind of attitude is what Gary Smalley calls "misplaced expectations."[1] If you expect your spouse to meet all your needs and expectations, you are most likely going to be unhappy. Smalley says, "Don't expect the other person to be your solution."[2] If you haven't learned this yet, it's time to understand that *you can't look to others to always make you happy.* Only God, not another human being, can meet all your needs. The decisions and choices you make determine greatly how circumstances will affect your life and relationships. A friend of mine has a statement in his notebook that says, "I can't change her, but I can change the way I react to her."

Remembering this is a good method for controlling the relational disease called "if only."

I have found that when the "if only's" overtake me and I feel like having a pity party for myself, the best way for me to control it is by doing a mental exercise of *walking in the shoes of my spouse*. When I truly try to get inside what makes Cathy the way she is, it is much easier for me to accept her strengths and faults. When I walk in her shoes it is easier to bestow grace and acceptance. The moment I put my needs before her needs is when I move right back into the "if only she would change" attitude. Empathy and forgiveness are very healthy ways of dealing with this issue. God is the giver of empathy and forgiveness. We are called to do the same thing for our spouses, even if it means lowering our expectations.

5. Choose Fun and Optimism

I love what Milton Berle was fond of saying: "Laughter is an instant vacation." It is amazing how a marriage can change for the better when there is fun and optimism in the relationship. It is true that this comes more naturally for some types of personalities. For the rest of us, we just have to work at this attitude a bit more intentionally.

A few years ago Cathy and I were reviewing our marriage. At least once a year, usually around our anniversary, we like to review our marriage. We ask questions like "What is working? What is not working?" and "What adjustments do we need to make?" We had to admit that it had been a rather intense year. We had been focused on raising three teenagers with lots of drama as well as trying to keep up with a growing ministry. Even though we were doing the regular date night and working on our relationship, it was more out of duty than joy. As I mentioned in chapter 6, both of us had to admit that we used to have a lot more fun than we had in this particular year.

We began remembering that one of the things that drew us together as a couple was all the fun things we did. We would spontaneously go play a game of tennis or call up friends to go out for pizza. We would drop what we were doing to spend a half day at the beach. But now so much of our life and focus was on balancing parenting, work responsibilities, and all the other tasks on our growing "to-do" list.

I had heard myself say to other people, "When we die, our *in* baskets will still be full; we have to be proactive about relationship priorities." The only problem was Cathy and I had become caught up in the tasks of life, and our relationship was in the dull cycle. And even though we knew that every marriage can have a season of difficulty, dryness, and dissatisfaction, we decided we needed to *do something* about ours.

We decided to make it the goal of our marriage as well as our family to have more fun. We began instituting family fun days and family fun movie nights. Cathy and I got out the calendar and decided we would schedule more fun into our marriage. We planned a couple of one-night trips away from home and bought tickets to a local theater group. We decided to take more walks with the dog and sit down together and watch our dearly beloved California Angels play on TV.

Interestingly enough the fun activities didn't eliminate any of the things on our to-do list. If there were problems and issues we needed to tackle, they were still there, but because there was a foundation of a bit more fun and optimism back in our life, we could take on the issues with a *different attitude*. I love what someone once said, "Think big thoughts, but relish small pleasures."[3] Small pleasures make for strong marriages. My experience says we just have to work on being more fun, because for most of us caught up in the fast pace of life, it doesn't come naturally.

Marriages where optimism is a main ingredient of the relationship do much better than those where pessimism rules. People generally learn to be optimists or pessimists in childhood and then carry one of these two basic attitudes throughout life. However, research shows that those whose outlook is pessimistic can reorient their thinking and view their world more optimistically.[4]

The Bible stresses the importance of thinking optimistically:

Finally, brothers, whatever is true, whatever is noble, whatever is right, whatever is pure, whatever is lovely, whatever is admirable—if anything is excellent or praiseworthy—think about such things. Whatever you have learned or received or heard from me, or seen in me—put it into practice. And the God of peace will be with you. (Philippians 4:8–9)

Remember, you can't change what has happened to you in the past, but you can take steps to ensure a better tomorrow. Here is how I personally work on my spiritual foundation for optimism and faith. I call it the Power of Daily.

THE POWER OF D.A.I.L.Y.

Over the years my attitude—and as a result my marriage—has been strengthened by the simplest of thoughts: *Live one day at a time*. This thought actually came from Jesus. In the Sermon on the Mount He instructs us: "Therefore do not be anxious about tomorrow, for tomorrow will be anxious for itself. Let the day's own trouble be sufficient for the day" (Matthew 6:34 RSV). In other words, *Live one day at a time*. I believe the secret to having the right attitude in life, faith, and marriage is found in those words.

I sat in a meeting in Chicago with several people. One man shared about his wife dying of cancer at age fifty a few months before. Another person talked about recovering from alcoholism and the battle they were facing with this addiction. One of the women talked about her bouts with depression and how paralyzed she felt in her marriage and family. Several shared their marriage problems and financial struggles. What made this meeting so interesting was that these people were all *key Christian leaders* in the world of youth and family ministry. They wrote the books I have read and been influenced by on these subjects. They speak at the same conferences at which I speak. I interview them on my radio show. Yet here they were, sharing their pain. Let's be honest; all people struggle with relational pain. Most people suffer with some type of a problem. Marriages break and bruise and sometimes bust apart.

We want the best marriage possible, but sometimes we aren't willing to work at even being polite to our spouse.

Those friends of mine are just like you and me. We are open, vulnerable, blocked, and closed. We have victories and defeats in life because, well, we are human. We live our lives as a bundle of contradictions. We want the best marriage possible, but sometimes we aren't willing to work at even being polite to our spouse. In the midst of all of this, God gives us the strength to live one day at a time. We can handle most anything that comes our way if we take on each day as a gift from God and rely upon His strength for the day.

In the Old Testament, the psalmist affirms, "This is the day the Lord has made; let us rejoice and be glad in it" (Psalm 118:24). In the Bible, it is absolutely amazing to read what God did (and can do) in *one day*. In one day:

* *He created the earth.*

* *He parted the Red Sea.*

* *He raised Jesus from the dead to bring eternal life.*

"This is the day the Lord has made; let us rejoice and be glad in it." There is such power in those words. When I can acknowledge that God created my day, I can rejoice and be grateful for it. I can't do much about what happened yesterday or last week, and I don't have as much control over tomorrow as I would like. But I can decide that *for this one day* I am going to seek God first, honor Cathy with extraordinary love, serve and love my kids, and do the best I can at work. I have enough strength for this day.

The acrostic D.A.I.L.Y. has helped me work on my attitude about life on a daily basis. I will have to admit that there are days when I get sidetracked and lose focus, but when I am focused on living one day at a time my life works much better. It takes discipline and discipleship. But the results are the foundation of a fulfilled life, meaningful marriage, and closer relationship with God. Let's break it down to see what the letters stand for.

DECIDE TO FOLLOW GOD DAILY

To decide to follow God is an act of the will. Sometimes it is an hourly or minute-by-minute decision. It is always a matter of choice and discipline. I love the advice Paul gave to Timothy: "Discipline yourself for the purpose of godliness" (see 1 Timothy 4:8 NASB). The Christian life and a Christ-honoring marriage is more than finding Jesus. It is *following* Jesus. Following Jesus is not a one-time spectacular event, but rather a one-day-at-a-time, somewhat ordinary and unspectacular commitment. The same is true for a healthy marriage. Marriage is sharing the mundane together. It is going through the daily routines of life, but being proactive about our daily commitment.

You make choices every day. You can choose joy over frustration and optimism over pessimism. Choose harmony in your marriage over tension. Choose affirmation over criticism. Choose belief over doubts. Choose healthy living over practices that make you vulnerable to sickness. Every day you can choose God over yourself.

A friend of mine told me that his schedule was brutal, and he found himself complaining to whoever would listen. Finally another good friend of his gently said, "But you scheduled yourself!" I've seen too many people who have no problem going to the doctor and paying to fix an illness, but these same people are not about to change the lifestyle that caused their problem in the first place. Your attitude is one day away from being in the right place to help your life and your marriage.

ADORE GOD DAILY

How does adoring God daily affect our life and marriage? The Bible says, "[The Lord] inhabitest the praises of [his people]" (Psalm 22:3 KJV). Adoration and praise remind us that God is in charge and we are not. Adoration fills our minds and thoughts with a God-honoring sense of gratefulness. When I am taking the time to adore God, it is much easier to honor Cathy. Adoration gives you a proper perspective on your life and circumstances.

If you have trouble doing this on a regular basis, then turn off the radio and listen to praise music. Sing in the shower. Do whatever it takes to build praise and thanksgiving into your day. Try reading five psalms and one chapter from Proverbs each day for a month. In one month you will have completed the entire books of Psalms and Proverbs; you'll also have an incredible amount of praise and adoration in your head. You can tell a great deal about a person's spiritual life from the amount and depth of praise and adoration they give to God. It is really difficult to have a bitter attitude toward your spouse while you have a heart full of adoration toward God.

IN THE WORD DAILY

As I mentioned in another chapter, the Bible is not a marriage handbook, but within the words of Scripture we find keys to a healthy marriage and a right attitude. In Psalm 119:105 we read: "Your word is a lamp to my feet and a light for my path." You may be thinking, *What does reading the Bible have to do with having more intimacy in my marriage?*

Actually, the Bible will give you the knowledge and inspiration to have a much healthier lifestyle and that will in turn produce a better marriage. Also most things we read won't last, but the words of Scripture are eternally true. Here's how Peter put it: "All [people] are like grass, and all their glory is like the flowers of the field; the grass withers and the flowers fall, but the word of the Lord stands forever" (1 Peter 1:24–25).

In 1986, I made a commitment to read through the entire Bible every year. There are days that I don't remember much of what I read, but this discipline has been important in sustaining me spiritually. One of the wisest decisions I will ever make to transform my attitude and marriage is taking ten or fifteen minutes a day to read the Bible. I find it helpful to use the *One Year Bible;* it is arranged in such a way that each day I have an Old Testament, New Testament, Psalms, and Proverbs text. I am always amazed how each time I pick up the Scripture there seems to be a truth that was just the thing I needed for the day.

One of the greatest favors you could do for your spouse is to read a portion of Scripture daily. God's will for your life and marriage is found in the Bible—not in the newspaper. I have found myself at times spending more time with the daily news than the daily Word. But the news doesn't help me bring a better attitude to my marriage . . . the Word does.

LOVE OTHERS DAILY

People with a right kind of attitude are people who are centered on others, not themselves. If I have an attitude of loving and serving my wife, then our relationship is strong. This doesn't mean we should be a doormat for our spouse, but it does mean we should be a servant. If you are struggling in your relationship with your spouse or with your life purpose, then stop thinking about you and your problems and take the action step to love others.

A friend of mine told me a story about a woman who had been in ill health for several years. She went to many different doctors, but none of them could find anything physically wrong with her. Whenever she could find a listening ear this woman would complain about her health, her lazy husband, and her grown kids who hardly ever kept in touch with her. (It's always amazing to me how a negative person seldom figures out that people are not clamoring to come around them because of their self-centered negativity.) Eventually she took her ill health and complaints to a very wise family doctor.

This gentleman listened to her complaints and gave her a thorough checkup. He then asked her to come into his office where he had written out a prescription. He handed it to her and said, "I think this will work for most of what you have wrong with you." It read: *Do something nice for someone else for fourteen days in a row and then come back and see me.*

She was angry with him and wanted him to prescribe some medication instead. He replied, "My friend, medication will not cure your health or those poor family relationships you were talking about." She was so mad that she told the doctor she wasn't going to pay him for his services. He said that was fine, but he challenged her again to follow his prescription. After all, what could it hurt? She was already miserable.

She finally decided to take his advice and found ways to do something loving for others for the next two weeks. She visited a lonely widow and brought her flowers, volunteered to baby-sit for a young mother's children, and brought a meal to a sick woman from her church. She even decided that she would be nicer to her husband and not complain to him. She bought him a new shirt and wrote him a nice note. She called her grown children and asked if there was anything she could do to help them out. She even wrote a small check to each of her grand-children.

Two weeks later she walked back into the physician's office and humbly thanked him for his wonderful advice. Doing something nice for someone else every day had changed her outlook. She even offered to pay him for his services!

Life is not meant to be all that complicated. Sure we have problems, but often our attitude is transformed and our relation-ships are strengthened when we concentrate on loving others with no strings attached. As we love others daily, we are really *loving and obeying God.* I like how the apostle John describes how we should love: "Little children, let us not love with word or with tongue, but in deed and truth" (1 John 3:18 NASB). Actions speak louder than words. Don't be surprised if loving actions not only bless the person you are serving but change your attitude as well.

YAHWEH REIGNS FOREVER

I love this acrostic because as we daily decide to work on our attitude and our spiritual walk with God, the result will be God reigning in our life. Yahweh is one of the Old Testament names for God. He brought security and safety to the people of Israel, and He still brings security and safety to people everywhere. When we allow our spiritual lives to align with God's ways, the result is that our marriage will be stronger and more filled with A.W.E. than we ever imagined. There are no perfect marriages, just as there are no perfect people this side of heaven. However, when someone focuses on having the right attitude with God every day, his or her marital relationship will be radically changed for the better.

ATTITUDE IS EVERYTHING

QUESTIONS FOR ME

1. What one "attitude adjustment" could I make in my life that would set the tone for a more intimate relationship with my spouse?

2. How would practicing "The Power of Daily" help me in every area of my life, especially my attitude?

QUESTIONS FOR US

1. Rate how you are doing in your marital relationship with these points from the chapter: 1 (needs major attention) to 10 (extremely satisfied).

	Me	*You*
• Stop complaining		
• Show gratitude		
• Practice the Golden Rule		
• Control the "if only's"		
• Choose fun and optimism		

2. What can *we* do to execute a better attitude in our marriage?

HEART-TO-HEART HOMEWORK
AFFIRMATION BOMBARDMENT

Write down twenty encouraging and affirming comments about your spouse. Then take the time to look him/her in the eyes and offer these words as a gift of affirmation.

1.

2.

3.

4.

5.

6.

7.

8.

9.

10.

11.

12.

13.

14.

15.

16.

17.

18.

19.

20.

Growing Toward Spiritual Intimacy

"We have never been what you would call 'spiritual giants,' but we did get married hoping for God's presence in our lives and in our family. We surely haven't done it right all the time, but it seems like we did make an effort. Today, however, I don't feel connected to my husband, and I definitely don't feel a spiritual connection to him." Those were the words of a woman who was telling me her story after one of our conferences. Her marriage wasn't on the rocks, but she was realizing that they had become so busy with kids, mortgages, work, school, and so many other things that they were missing the spiritual connection that she hoped for when they first got married.

Other couples tell me that they didn't have much of a spiritual bent when they got married, and I am amazed at how many people tell me that they are spiritually motivated, but their spouse has little or no interest. Regardless of where you are at as a couple in the spiritual intimacy department, there is probably room for growth. For the majority of people who read this book, spiritual intimacy is perhaps the least developed area of their marital relationship.

Jesus described marriage on a very spiritual level: "'A man leaves his father and mother and is joined to his wife, and the two are united into one.' Since they are no longer two but one, let no one separate them, for God has joined them together" (Matthew 19:5–6 NLT). It's very possible that those verses were read at your wedding. And for most of us, those words would be the desire of our hearts. When you look at this beautiful statement, isn't that what you would hope for in your relationship? A man and woman *leave* their parents to become *united*. They become literally *one flesh*. You and your spouse are definitely two individuals, but if you are like most people, you have a desire to become more *intimate* emotionally, physically, and yes, even spiritually.

Jesus' words "Let no one separate" expresses our desire for God's presence to be in our relationship. But to want something and to have it are two different things. We may desire a spiritual connection as a couple, but sadly it is usually the least developed area of the relationship. It takes time, open communication, humility, grace, and a desire for spiritual growth for any couple to grow together spiritually. Even then, there are major blocks we must overcome to achieve it. It goes back to one of the main themes running through this entire book, and that is intentionality. Before we can put much of a plan together, we have to look briefly at a few of the things that can block our spiritual intimacy. They aren't that much different from what blocks other types of intimacy.

BLOCKS TO GROWING TOGETHER SPIRITUALLY

Growing together spiritually is not our natural bent. Most people had very few role models in this area; maybe their own parents' marriage was less than helpful in setting an example. And of course, even with good role models and knowing what we should do in terms of building spiritual intimacy, we often let other less-important things get in the way. Cathy and I have tried every "spiritual growth marriage program" available. They are all good, but too often something gets in the way.

Before you create your own plan that will work for you, you'll have to ask this question: What is holding us back as a couple? Some people can answer that question easily, while others just don't know how to get past some of the roadblocks. If you know exactly what to do, then skip this part and move on to creating a plan to grow closer together and connect on a deeper level spiritually. If you aren't sure why you seem to be blocked, read on!

BUSYNESS

This is beginning to sound like a broken record, but busyness is perhaps the main issue to blocking intimacy of all kinds—especially spiritual intimacy. When Cathy and I were first married we had high hopes that we would have a deep, connected spiritual life together. We assumed it would happen just because we wanted it to happen.

> **We assumed it would happen just because we wanted it to happen.**

Our first excuse was that we worked very different hours and couldn't find the right time. I wanted to spend some time with Cathy in the morning and she is more of an evening person. I was too tired in the evening and she wasn't breathing when I wanted to spend time with her and God in the morning. Next came a very demanding ministry position, then a child, then more kids, then crisis-mode living and too many plates to spin. We were both tired and distracted and kept making excuses. Pretty soon we had to just admit that in our busyness of life, it was easy to miss being intentional about working on our spiritual intimacy.

Why is it that couples can feel closer on a vacation or a

church retreat? There really is a simple answer to that question: We slow down and focus on each other. Somehow we have to figure it out in the midst of our life and make it a priority and part of our everyday routine.

LOW-LEVEL ANGER

If we are honest about our relationship with our spouse, it is very easy to have at least low-level anger at all times. As I have said before, "You can be angry at your spouse and teenagers 24/7/365." Relationships are bumpy. Without good communication and healthy conflict resolutions we build up resentments and minor irritations that escalate more ·than they should. Pretty soon we are carrying around a whole lot of baggage called anger, annoyance, fury, as well as other resentments. When these issues are left to boil, it is very difficult to come together spiritually.

The Bible says, "Do not let the sun go down while you are still angry" (Ephesians 4:26). That's good and right advice. However, sometimes it's easier with the big concerns that are more obvious. We have a tendency to let the little annoyances simmer and build up into what become larger-than-life issues because we don't deal with them right away.

One couple told me that they have had to learn to pray together *even if* they are angry. First, they try to deal with the conflict. If they still can't get resolution, then they take a moment, hold hands, and pray together. The only rule is that they can't preach at each other in their prayers. Low-level anger can put the spiritual fires out as quickly as anything else.

LACK OF FORGIVENESS

When your spouse has done something against you and you are unable to forgive him or her, you are blocking spiritual intimacy. Forgiveness is a necessary ingredient for a right relationship with both God and your spouse. We live in a society that has taught us to have conditional love, and that kind of love harbors a lack of forgiveness. This may be a major issue for your relationship; if you can't resolve it, you probably won't grow spiritually.

Jerry was a youth worker in a church who had what he called an "emotional affair" with a co-worker. He and the co-worker had lost their boundaries and they were definitely violating their values. Finally one night he came clean with his wife. He told her everything and told her he needed help. During the crisis, his wife was wonderful. She was understanding, firm, helpful, and supportive. Jerry got the help he needed, and the co-worker ended up changing jobs. Two marriages were saved, and the potential heartbreak for the children and families of both couples was averted.

However, after one of our Ministry and Marriage conferences, Jerry's wife came to me and told me about her ongoing struggle. She had been through so much, and she had done a great job. She wanted to talk because she still wasn't connecting with Jerry spiritually. The more we talked, the more I began to see that she had never *forgiven* Jerry for abandoning her emotionally. Jerry had asked for forgiveness from both God and his wife, and it looked like he had truly repented of his behavior. Although she wanted to forgive him, she was still harboring a lack of mercy. Her resentment was affecting their relationship, especially their spiritual intimacy.

As much as Jerry was in the wrong, it was his wife who would have to deal with her lack of forgiveness in order for their relationship to grow. Most of the time this kind of situation is not a quick fix. It often takes seeking out some counseling from a pastor or Christian therapist to work through all the issues. But it was important to their marriage that Jerry's wife be willing to do what it took to find forgiveness in her heart. Only then could they hope to flourish in the area of spiritual intimacy.

LACK OF RESPECT

Isn't it amazing that two fairly normal and actually pretty nice people can get married and treat each other like *complete idiots?* Someone once said, "If you took all the problems in your neighborhood and threw them out in the street, after sifting through them, you would probably pick up your *own problems* and take them back home with you." No one would disagree with the biblical statement "All have sinned and fall short of the glory of God" (Romans 3:23).

Marriage brings out both the best in us . . . and the worst. Cathy knows me at my very worst. She has every reason not to respect me and call me a hypocrite. Every married person can say the same about his or her spouse. Perhaps your spouse has some major issues, such as addictions, and it is very difficult to respect their behavior. I am not telling you to look the other way in major issues like that. But in the general areas of human frailty we need to overlook a lot if we want to grow together spiritually. It doesn't take perfection to achieve spiritual intimacy—it takes transparency and integrity. You can still respect people without approving of their sin. The biblical term *grace* means *unmerited* favor. God gives us grace, and we in turn should give it to our spouse.

The Jews brought a woman to Jesus who was caught engaging in adultery. No doubt she was deeply ashamed as they discussed her fate in her presence.

"Teacher," they said to Jesus, "this woman was caught in the very act of adultery. The law of Moses says to stone her. What do you say?" They were trying to trap him into saying something they could use against him, but Jesus stooped down and wrote in the dust with his finger. They kept demanding an answer, so he stood up again and said, "All right, stone her. But let those who have never sinned throw the first stones!" Then he stooped down again and wrote in the dust.

When the accusers heard this, they slipped away one by one, beginning with the oldest, until only Jesus was left in the middle of the crowd with the woman. Then Jesus stood up again and said to her, "Where are your accusers? Didn't even one of them condemn you?" "No, Lord," she said. And Jesus said, "Neither do I. Go and sin no more" (John 8:4–11 NLT).

Jesus treated this woman who had definitely been caught in serious sin with amazing respect. He knew the law and did not gloss over her transgression. But he did not look down on her or treat her with scorn. His respect, gentleness, and mercy (while still admonishing her to leave this kind of behavior behind) is a good model for us as we interact with our spouse. Unlike Jesus, we can't afford to be too smug as we point out other people's faults since *we are just as guilty* as they are. If we are serious about building spiritual intimacy in our marriage we need to be careful. If we demonstrate a lack of respect and disdain for our partner we'll forfeit the gains we are seeking.

SPIRITUAL WARFARE

I don't know about you, but I believe there is a spiritual battle that takes place for the soul of every marriage. Satan opposes spiritual growth in couples for obvious reasons. I can't speak for Satan, but I believe he never hesitates to go for

> **I believe there is a spiritual battle that takes place for the soul of every marriage.**

the jugular, which is your marriage. Sure the power of evil brings sin into our lives, but Satan also does something else that is more subtle: He causes a couple to settle for a lack of spiritual intimacy. He knows there is heavenly power against him that can pay dividends for generations to come when a couple walks together spiritually!

At a conference recently I asked five hundred couples in ministry if any of them believed they had witnessed spiritual warfare taking place in their marriage. All of them raised their hands! As we began to share about spiritual warfare, they said they needed God's power *the most* when dealing with marital challenges. The Bible is clear: "Greater is He who is in you than he who is in the world" (1 John 4:4 NASB). James 4:7–8 gives us the strategy for winning in this battle: "Submit yourselves . . . to God. Resist the devil, and he will flee from you. Come near to God and he will come near to you." Don't underestimate the spiritual battle taking place for the spiritual intimacy of your marriage. You can't expect your marriage to grow spiritually merely by circumstance and chance. You must be *intentional* about refreshing your marriage spiritually.

REFRESHING YOUR MARRIAGE SPIRITUALLY

As I have mentioned throughout this book, intentionality is the key. There isn't anyone reading this book that would not *begin with a plan* if he or she was starting a business. Yet most couples not only do not have a plan to grow together toward spiritual intimacy . . . they don't even talk about it. Often it is a back-burner topic at best.

Yet when I discuss this topic in conferences or on my radio program, many people say with almost a far-off yearning look, "I wish my spouse and I were closer spiritually." It's not going to happen without a plan. To quote one of my favorite movies, *What About Bob?*, it will best be done with "baby steps." It is very rare for a relationship to move from lacking spiritually to strong growth overnight. It takes nurturing and pruning over time to have a beautiful garden; in the same way, it takes time and careful cultivation to grow toward spiritual intimacy. And it won't happen by osmosis. It will happen when one or both of the spouses start by *planting the seeds* of spiritual growth.

You can start the process by praying daily for your spouse and your relationship. Paul's advice to Timothy was to "discipline yourself for the purpose of godliness" (1 Timothy 4:7). I'm not talking about hours of prayer, but simply a daily time (however short) to pray for your spouse. Give your relationship to God. Pray for your spouse's needs and seek God's will for how you can serve your spouse. Even this one simple act of daily disciplined prayer for your spouse will make a difference. As you pray, look for an opportunity to create a plan. The old adage

"Fail to plan, plan to fail" is so true when couples desire to experience spiritual growth together.

PRAY TOGETHER

If your spouse is open to it, pray together daily. If your spouse is not very spiritually motivated, then keep prayer very short and do it at a meal or another time that seems less intimidating. I know one couple who started praying together every day with the wife simply saying, "God, thank you for our food. Thank you for the children. Thank you so much for Jack. Help us to be a God-honoring couple and family. Amen."

One day, after months of that prayer, Jack said, "Let me pray, too." He said, "God, I'm not much of a pray-er but I agree with Janet, and thanks for Janet's heart for you. Amen, again!" After a while the kids got involved too. After a year Jack and Janet were feeling more comfortable praying together.

Our pastor made an amazing statement one day in church. He said, "I have never seen one couple go through with a divorce after praying together, on their knees, every day for a month." Praying together is the glue that binds our hearts together and focuses us on God's power in our marriage and family. The mistake some couples make is that they start with goals that are too high, and they expect too much too soon. Praying together is a bit like going to the gym. We may be excited about getting started on a physical fitness program, but the long-lasting results happen only after time and discipline.

The Swiss psychiatrist Dr. Paul Tournier wrote,

> It is only when a husband and wife pray together before God that they find the secret of true harmony: that the difference in their temperaments, their ideas, and their tastes enriches their home instead of endangering it. When each of the marriage partners seeks quietly before God to see his own faults, recognizes his sin, and asks for the forgiveness of the other, marital problems are no more. They learn to become absolutely honest with each other. This is the price to be paid

if partners very different from each other are to combine their gifts instead of setting them against each other.[1]

Praying together can bring about spiritual intimacy and it can also restore a broken marriage. Praying together can strengthen a marriage that is lacking in communication and intimacy. It is certainly worth a try. The saying is true: "Couples who pray together, stay together."

WORSHIP TOGETHER REGULARLY

As I've already mentioned, the Scripture teaches us that the Lord inhabits the praises of his people (Psalm 22:3 KJV). If you want the Lord to inhabit your relationship, then a natural ingredient is *worshiping together*. Unfortunately, some couples don't have the benefit of worshiping together. Perhaps one works or just won't go to church. This is an area to keep on your prayer list; look for ways to find meaning together when you can.

I know of a husband who agreed to go to church with his wife once a month. Instead of nagging or condemning about the other three weeks, she made a big deal out of that one morning a month by serving fun food and turning it into a pleasurable event. Within the year he was going most Sundays. Today, after many years, he is a *leader* in their church. Set the tone for a good experience. Pray for God's Spirit to inhabit your worship.

DEVELOP A REGULAR SPIRITUAL GROWTH TIME TOGETHER

It isn't easy to discipline yourselves as a couple to spend regular time together focusing on your spirituality. Even though Cathy and I speak and write on this subject, we have struggled throughout the thirty-one years of our marriage in this area. We have tried reading books together and doing Bible study booklets. We have listened to CDs and watched videos together on spiritual growth. We have tried to have a daily time and a weekly time to focus on our spiritual growth. Like so many others, it hasn't always worked for us.

Sometimes the reasons were found in the list of blocks to spiritual growth found earlier in this chapter. We always meant well, but it just didn't seem to last. Finally we found something that worked for us. We call it our *Weekly Time*. It's really rather simple, and for some it may be too short, but it has worked for us. We have shared it with thousands of people and some are now actually more faithful at it than we are. It started from our need to focus together spiritually, but we didn't want to just do another Bible study or devotional. Both Cathy and I are disciplined with our own daily devotional time, and adding one more devotional as a couple just wasn't working. That's when we came up with the following.

Jim and Cathy's Weekly Time

* *Devotional time of the week*

* *Greatest joy of the week*

* *Greatest struggle of the week*

* *An affirmation*

* *A wish or a hope*

* *Physical goals*

* *Prayer*

* *Book of the month*

We decided to take the pressure off of meeting more often than once a week, and just share with each other what we had been learning from our own time with the Lord. Sometimes that takes a few minutes and other times it is a bit deeper. Then we move to the greatest joy of the week. For Cathy, it is almost always something about one of our kids. For me, it might be about our kids or a ministry experience.

We then share our greatest struggle. Yes, there have been

times when Cathy has said, "The greatest struggle of the week is you, Jim!" Then we may have a conversation about the struggle before we can move back into our devotional time.

We each share an affirmation about the other. Next, it's a wish or a hope we share. I don't remember why we added that section, but it is a catch-all for good conversation. When Cathy's father was near death, we talked about her relationship with him. Other times it has been a hope for a vacation weekend. Then we deal with our physical goals. Since Scripture is clear that our bodies are temples of the Holy Spirit (1 Corinthians 6:19), we try to work on our physical goals. If you were looking at both Cathy and me in person, you would see that she does a better job in this area than I do! However, that weekly checkup is a very good accountability factor for both of us.

Then we pray. Lately, we have spent some time praying on our knees. It is a time of drawing close to God, and it has also become a time of drawing closer together. I love this time of communication. There is nothing magical about this spiritual exercise, but it works for us. The important issue is to find something that works for both you and your spouse. You'll also notice above that I included "book of the month" as one of the points under our plan. It is a great idea. We tried it, and it didn't work for us. But maybe when life slows down a bit, we'll find it helpful.

TIME WITH OTHER COUPLES

You will notice that a common theme in what they call the "temptation narratives" in the Bible is isolation. Even when Satan tempted Jesus, he took Him to the wilderness and isolated Him from other people. Far too many couples are isolated from any other replenishing relationships. Who has access to your life as a couple? I believe we need at least three types of spiritual and relational accountability. We need mentors, peer support, and whenever possible, we need to be mentoring other couples.

Do you have mentors in your life as a couple? I know for us,

Cathy and I had very few role models when we first got married. We didn't know many couples we wanted to imitate in our own marriage. One day we were talking about the need to find mentors for our marriage, and a couple from our church came to our mind. They had successfully raised three kids and had been married for a number of years. We asked if we could come by and ask them some questions about building a God-honoring marriage.

If we would have said, "Will you mentor us?" they might have said, "No, we don't see ourselves as mentors." Fortunately, we didn't give them the option to turn us down. We simply asked if we could get together. The meal time and con-

Far too many couples are isolated from any other replenishing relationships.

versation was so pleasant and helpful that we asked if we could get together again sometime. Today, this couple would probably say they have been mentors to us, but it didn't start that way in their minds.

We are most fortunate to have couples on our board of directors at HomeWord who we would consider mentors as well. These are not people who have every aspect of their lives together. However, they are a bit older and wiser than we are and are open to sharing their lives with us. If you don't have a mentor couple, I suggest you begin to talk about who might help motivate you to grow spiritually and through their lives show you how to be more effective in your marriage and family.

We also believe strongly in peer relationships. I meet with a group of four other men on Tuesday mornings, as well as every couple of months with a friend whom I respect greatly. We share the hard questions and challenge each other in our marriages, spiritual life, child-rearing, integrity, and being faithful in our calling. Cathy and I were in a couples' group for several years, and even though each session wasn't on marriage, it seemed like whatever we were studying in that group came back to our marriages and families. I learned much from how other couples approached their relationships. We often say that this particular group helped us raise our kids and taught us more about marriage than any book we have ever read.

Then how about mentoring a younger couple? Your church probably has a mentoring program for newlyweds or younger couples. It might be something as formal as going through a book together or as informal as sharing a few meals a year with a younger couple. I know for Cathy and me, when we are in conversation with another couple about our marriage, we are much more intentional about working our spiritual growth plan.

OTHER IDEAS

As we looked at refreshing our marriage spiritually I mentioned that we all need a plan. When a couple is living with the same set of blueprints, they do so much better. The above ideas are a major part of Cathy's and my plan. You will want to create your own. It has to work for you and for your situation. I know couples who have taken a five-hour solo/Sabbath time regularly to rest, pray, read inspirational literature, hike, and then come back together to talk about their experience. They do it almost every week. Sure it takes time, but by the looks of their marriage it is definitely worth the investment.

Another couple I know plans two retreats a year. One of the retreats they do is a getaway together. They go away to a cabin in the mountains or a place at the beach. At different times they have read books together, listened to tapes, or followed a Bible study booklet. Their time together is spent taking extended time to walk, rest, pray, relate, and focus on their marriage and their yearly goals. They also participate in one retreat a year with other couples. They attend a marriage conference or go to a retreat center where the topic is marriage and family.

These are some of the people we would consider "mentors" in our lives. They do really well in the area of spiritual intimacy because they invest heavily in their marriage. Another couple I know reads at least one book a year together on marriage. They got started doing this because in the business world he was reading about three books a year on his specific business to keep up with his line of work. One day it dawned on him that he had never read even one marriage book to help keep his marriage in shape, so as a couple they instituted the "once-a-year book plan." They choose the book together and then plan when they are going to read it. One year they went on a long driving trip and read a book on sexuality *out loud* to each other during the trip.

Spiritual growth and intimacy is like anything else. It takes time and commitment. It is more about training than trying, and just like the Scripture says, you will reap what you sow (Galatians 6:7–8). Don't shortchange yourself or your spouse by not focusing on spiritual intimacy. At the end of your life you won't be focused on your IRA retirement plan, the kind of house you live in, or what your bank account looks like. You will be interested in a right relationship with God and a right relationship with your loved ones. Since that is doing relationships with an eternal perspective, why not start sooner rather than later?

GROWING TOWARD SPIRITUAL INTIMACY

QUESTIONS FOR ME

1. Which of the following blocks to spiritual intimacy affect your life the most?

   * *busyness*

   * *low-level anger*

   * *lack of forgiveness*

   * *lack of respect*

   * *spiritual warfare*

   * *other* _____

2. What can I personally do to bring more spiritual intimacy to our relationship?

QUESTIONS FOR US

1. Share with each other your answer to question #1 from Questions for Me.
2. Complete this sentence: If I could receive more spiritual intimacy from you it would be in the area of _____.

HEART-TO-HEART HOMEWORK
OUR SPIRITUAL GROWTH PLAN

Create together a simple plan to enhance your spiritual relationship as a couple. Remember to keep it short and simple so you don't get too overwhelmed.

Put down on paper things like:

* *Pray daily.*

* *Worship together weekly.*

* *Join a couples group.*

* *Participate in a marriage or spiritual retreat.*

* *Develop a regular spiritual growth time together.*

To get you started, how about taking a few minutes and working through the Weekly Time together discussed on pages 163-164.

Our Weekly Time

* *Devotional time of the week* (If you need an idea for this week, try reading through Ephesians 5:22–33.)

* *Greatest joy of the week*

* *Greatest struggle of the week*

* *An affirmation*

* *A wish or a hope*

* *Physical goals*

* *Prayer*

* *Book of the month*

chapter 10

Renewing and Reviewing Your Marriage Vows

Most people seldom think about their wedding vows, but they are incredibly important and sacred to your marriage. One of the great privileges and joys of my life is participating in the renewal of marriage vows. Often these kinds of ceremonies are actually more meaningful and more intentional than the first wedding ceremony. I have seen couples who have been married for twenty-five to fifty years weep with joy at the renewing of their vows. So often they tell me that they hardly remembered what happened the first time around.

I want to suggest that if you have stayed with me through this entire book that you consider *reviewing* your vows and then look for a time to *renew* your vows in a way that would be meaningful for you as a couple. If you have a video or audiotape of your wedding ceremony, I suggest you watch it together and listen to the beauty and wisdom of the ceremony and your vows to each other. Every wedding has a different style, and the words used in each wedding are always unique and special. Yet for most weddings, there are similar elements that make up the ceremony.

For most of us, we were not focused on the meaning of the ceremony when we got married. We were too distracted by all the details of the event and the people who attended. As time goes on, though, we begin to appreciate the beauty of an exceptional and meaningful service.

In this chapter I want to walk through a basic Christian wedding ceremony. Your particular ceremony was no doubt somewhat different, but perhaps some of the elements we will discuss can be helpful for you to *review* your vows and then possibly *renew* them. We won't look at every part of a service; we'll be focusing on the significance of some of the essential elements that make up a meaningful ceremony. (Please note that I am not using the proper names of some of these elements. This does not reflect one particular denomination or theological persuasion, but rather a Christian ceremony in general.)

THE TRADITIONAL CHRISTIAN WEDDING CEREMONY

The Audience and Wedding Party

Your wedding party and audience are your witnesses of a miracle that is taking place: Two people are becoming united to become *one*. They celebrate God's goodness with you, and can also hold you accountable as they witness your vows to each other before God, them, and yourselves.

Father and the Bride

The Bible is clear that "'A man will leave his father and mother and be united to his wife, and the two will become one flesh.' So they are no longer two, but one. Therefore what God has joined together, let man not separate" (Matthew 19:5–6).

In this act, you are leaving your family and uniting with your spouse to form a new family. You are acknowledging that you are one flesh, and the God who created the universe is present in joining you together. You are acknowledging God's presence and declaring that you will not be separated.

The Vows of Intent: Fidelity

_____, *will you have* _____ *to be your husband/wife and will you pledge your life to him/her, in all love and honor, in all duty and service, in all faith and tenderness, to love him/her and cherish him/her, according to the ordinance of God, in the holy bond of marriage?*
(I will.)

In most traditional church ceremonies the vows of intent happen while you are standing at the steps before you come up to the altar. The significance of this act is that you pledge your intent to be one before you move up to the "Holy of Holies" for the actual vows and exchange of rings to each other before God and your witnesses.

In a sense, these vows are an invitation to become one in this ceremony. You are pledging mutual submission (Ephesians 5:22–33) to each other, saying that you will submit to one another and be a servant lover. Your commitment is to show honor to your spouse—to "Outdo one another in showing honor" (Romans 12:10 RSV). In this vow of fidelity, you are telling your spouse that you are going to include God and His ordinances in your marriage. It is amazing how these few words bring so much richness to our vows.

The Welcome and Prayer

Although most churches use other words for this part of the service, it is basically a time to acknowledge God's existence in the wedding ceremony and to call upon His presence for the ceremony and the marriage relationship.

The Message

"Love is patient and kind. Love is not jealous or boastful or proud or rude. Love does not demand its own way. Love is not irritable, and it keeps no record of when it has been wronged. It is never glad about injustice but rejoices whenever the truth wins out. Love never gives up, never loses faith, is always hopeful, and endures through every circumstance" (1 Corinthians 13:4–7 NLT).

Of course, not every message or sermonette in a wedding ceremony uses this beautiful passage written by the apostle Paul to the Corinthian believers. But often the message does focus on the unconditional love of God for the couple and the love the couple has for each other. Marriage is a wonderful reminder of the faithfulness of God and the faithfulness of the couple to each other and to God. The passage above is the *goal* for a relationship and, in a sense, is a blueprint for a great marriage. As we have mentioned in other parts of the book, you can't have a great marriage living with two different sets of blueprints.

The Vows of Commitment: Faithfulness

I, _____, take you, _____, to be my husband/wife. I promise and covenant before God and these witnesses to be your loving and faithful wife/husband—in plenty and in want, in sickness and in health, in joy and in sorrow, in good times and hard times, with God's grace and strength, as long as we both shall live.

In many ways, these are the most sacred of vows to each other. They are the vows of commitment and faithfulness to each other no matter what the circumstance. It is a personal vow. As you know, many people are choosing to write their own vows, which I like to see happen. Yet at the same time, these more traditional words say so much with just a few lines. This commitment is what often gets broken in our "what's in it for me" world. It is a vow to be faithfully loving in good times and hard times, while relying on God's grace and strength.

Exchange of Rings

This ring I give you as a symbol of our renewed pledge to our constant faith and abiding love.

The wedding ring is a symbol of God's unconditional love. God loves you, not for what you do, but for who you are . . . His child. The circle signifies the eternal perspective of God's unconditional love. When you place the ring on your spouse's finger, you are saying to God and the world that you will love your spouse with the same kind of unconditional love that God has for you. It is a symbol and seal of your love. You are also acknowledging that you will need His power to do it.

Communion

"For I received from the Lord what I also passed on to you: The Lord Jesus, on the night he was betrayed, took bread, and when he had given thanks, he broke it and said, 'This is my body, which is for you; do this in remembrance of me.' In the same way, after supper he took the cup, saying, 'This cup is the new covenant in my blood; do this, whenever you drink it, in remembrance of me.' For whenever you eat this bread and drink this cup, you proclaim the Lord's death until he comes" (1 Corinthians 11:23–26).

How appropriate that Communion (or the Eucharist, as some call it) is often the first act of marriage after the sealing of the marriage through the exchange of rings. In Communion we acknowledge our sinfulness and brokenness, bought at a price. The price of our salvation is, of course, the broken body and shed blood of Jesus Christ. In this most holy of acts, we once again acknowledge our need for Christ to form what some call "The Divine Triangle." The right kind of marriage is when not only two hearts and two souls are joined together to be one, but where Christ is an integral part of the relationship as well.

A Song of Joy

Most wedding ceremonies have music. Usually there are songs of joy proclaiming the miracle of God's love reigning in the life of the couple. There are often songs of praise and adoration welcoming God into the couple's life. A wedding is a joyful celebration of love and commitment.

Candle Lighting

When a couple takes two candles and then lights the center one, it is a symbol of two people becoming united to become one flesh. By this I am again reminded of the incredible miracle of God's goodness, creating oneness and unity out of two individual lives.

The Pronouncement

By the authority committed to me as a minister of the gospel of Jesus Christ, I declare _____ and _____ are now husband and wife; in the name of the Father, and of the Son, and of the Holy Spirit. Amen.

This is the declaration of the miracle of oneness. To many, this declaration by the pastor is a sign of God accepting this couple to become one in Him.

The Kiss

This is the symbol of love for each other. Romance, affection, and a commitment to be physical with no one else are all a part of the kiss. In that kiss the couple is saying, "We are each other's—and no one else's—for as long as we live."

The Introduction of Oneness

May I introduce to you, Mr. and Mrs. _____.
    You might have come to this ceremony as two, but you are

leaving as one. Again, the acknowledgement of unity to become one is evident in the introduction of your new name.

As you can see from this ceremony, each part of it is a very spiritual and meaningful part of your relationship. Reviewing and renewing your vows is a wonderful way to move toward spiritual intimacy. As you read over your vows from your own ceremony, you will see how often the A.W.E. factor discussed in this book is present in the words, symbolism, and the ceremony itself.

One couple I know made a copy of the words of their wedding ceremony and placed them in their bedroom as a reminder of their commitment. Even if you don't have a copy of your vows or the ceremony, it is never too late to recreate them as you renew your commitment to each other.

Creating an intimate marriage is both a privilege and a sacred duty. The good news is, you have all the resources you need. God, who ordained marriage in the first place, has promised to see you through. I pray that with His help your marriage will be full of A.W.E. from the moment you get up in the morning until you go to bed at night. Go back to where it all started and renew your pledge to the one you were so excited to marry. Be intentional. Be persistent. And in time, *enjoy all the blessings* that come with an intimate marriage!

If you stayed with me during this entire book, then I believe you are more than willing to invest heavily in your marriage. Even if you have a high-maintenance relationship, there is incredible hope for creating a more intimate marriage. I want to leave you with a couple of phrases from Scripture that have been a great source of encouragement in my life and marriage. *"Let us run with perseverance the race marked out for us." "Consider him who endured such opposition from sinful men, so that you will not grow weary and lose heart"* (Hebrews 12:1, 3).

The writer is talking about steadfast endurance. It reminds us not to bail out too early when marriage gets difficult, but rather to persevere and hold true to our commitments. I encourage you to stay focused and practice your priorities. You will not regret it because *the best years are yet to come.*

RENEWING AND REVIEWING YOUR MARRIAGE VOWS

QUESTIONS FOR ME

1. What part of your wedding ceremony was most meaningful to you on your wedding day? Is that still true today?

2. What part of your wedding vows and ceremony do you need to work on in your own life?

QUESTIONS FOR US

1. If you have an audiotape or video/DVD of your ceremony, review the entire ceremony. Review with each other the meaningful parts of the ceremony. (If you don't have a tape, then try to recreate your ceremony and review the meaningful parts.)

2. As a couple, discuss the possibility of renewing your vows either in a public ceremony or privately.

HEART-TO-HEART HOMEWORK
YOUR RENEWAL OF VOWS

Write out your own set of vows for renewal and share them with your spouse.

Questions and Answers

1. My husband isn't interested in leading our kids spiritually. Any suggestions?

This is a common issue in marriages. If your husband doesn't want to take the job, then the job is yours. I know one woman who was very frustrated that her husband was not doing his part in providing spiritual leadership in the home. She nagged him, scolded him, shamed him, and tried every kind of manipulation to motivate him toward taking it on. He wasn't much of a church attendee, and she was very upset with him about that too. She wanted me to talk with her husband.

I said, "Let me get this straight. Your husband isn't very spiritually motivated and you think the best way to bring him around to your idea of spiritual maturity is to be *negative* toward him? Since that hasn't worked (and frankly, I have never seen shame-based communication work in a situation like this, or any for that matter), how about trying another way?"

If your spouse isn't interested in taking on the spiritual leadership in your home, then you must take the lead. You can use what I like to call the K.I.S.S. Method. This stands for Keep It Short and Simple.

- *Pray daily with your kids.* Bedtime is a great time to offer a short prayer and, depending upon their age, sometimes a story (if they are small) or an opportunity to just talk (if they are older).

- *Pray at meals.* Ask the children to participate in prayers around the table. Never put your husband down in front of the kids, and include him whenever possible, if he feels comfortable.

- *Create a short weekly devotional time with the kids.* This isn't the time for long-winded lectures, but rather a time to focus on one Scripture or one topic. Kids learn best when they do the talking (not you). They will support what they help create, so let them plan the time. Keep it short, and ask your husband if he would like to join you and the kids. If he declines, just smile and say, "Okay."

- *Worship together at least weekly.* Whether your spouse attends and participates in it or not, worship together regularly. If your kids are old enough, help them get involved in a youth or children's group. Make the worship experience a positive event. After-church ice cream appointments, a short shopping spree, or time at the park can sometimes make the difference. If the kids are involved in a singing program at church, make sure they invite your spouse to hear them. But keep the invitation positive.

Pray for your spouse daily and treat him with respect. It was *your choice* to marry someone who was not spiritually motivated. The way to bring him closer to God is by honoring him with kindness and love. Remember that Paul's advice to the Roman believers was to "outdo one another in showing honor" (Romans 12:10 RSV).

2. My husband had an affair and now I am having trouble forgiving and forgetting. Is there hope?

Let me give you an illustration. You are walking down the street near your home and someone comes up behind you and hits you across the face with a two-by-four. You are broken and bloody. There is a possibility of healing, but you must get the help you need to heal. Figuratively, this is what happened to you when you found out your husband had broken his marriage vow to be true and faithful to you. The only difference is you don't have the scars on the outside of your body. Your pain is inside and out of sight from all except those who know your story.

Is it possible to forgive? The answer is a resounding *yes!* Is it easy? Absolutely not! I do know people who have actually faced the same experience you have and found a deeper and more intimate love together than they had ever experienced before in their marriage. I don't think they are the norm. I would add that all the people I know who have found forgiveness in their hearts have really had to roll up their sleeves and *work at it.*

The first question I would ask you is: Do you have it within you to work on the relationship? It is going to take a great deal of work and focus on your part. In fact, sometimes when a person has had an affair and they put it behind them, it is easier for them than for the spouse who was the victim of their unfaithfulness.

Of course, a major part of the trust issue rests with your spouse. Has he been *willing* to admit his destructive behavior and totally walk away from the other person? Just like an alcoholic who must never take a drink again, your husband must never be in touch again with the woman he had the affair with, period. Is he willing to be in an accountability relationship with at least one other man to help keep him from going down that destructive road again? Are you and your husband willing to seek the advice and counsel of a professional who can help repair the damage to your relationship? Is your husband willing to seek God's forgiveness and ongoing presence in your "new relationship"? If he is not willing to deal with any of these issues, then you will have a difficult time trusting him.

As for you, the Bible says, "Where there is no counsel, the people fall; but in the multitude of counselors there is safety" (Proverbs 11:14 NKJV). Seek the safety of wise counsel, and since it is your desire to forgive, walk very slowly toward reconciliation. If you are going to reconcile, you will need to forgive him or the relationship won't work. You can't keep holding his offense over his head for the rest of your life and expect much connection.

I can't speak for you. If Cathy was unfaithful, I would still want to reconcile. To be perfectly honest, for the first few years of our marriage, I might have closed the door to reconciliation. But after thirty-plus years, I believe I would move toward reconciliation first. Above all else, seek help. Don't suffer in silence.

3. *I was sexually abused as a child and haven't told anyone about it. Now I think it might be affecting my relationship with my husband.*

Sexual abuse is a trauma that will affect most aspects of your life, so your childhood sexual assault definitely will affect your relationship with your husband. I urge you to get the help you need to move toward healing. When I am doing any kind of premarital counseling I always ask the couple if there has been any kind of sexual, physical, or emotional abuse in their lives. I want them to understand that they must begin dealing with their pain of abuse *before* they marry. This is not a secret to hide from your spouse. It is also not a secret to keep inside you. Here is what I tell people who have been victims of sexual abuse.

- *It's not your fault; it is always the fault of the abuser.* Far too many people feel so much shame that they actually blame themselves for what happened. You were a victim. You can't keep blaming yourself.

* *Seek help—do not suffer in silence.* It sounds like you have kept this traumatic experience to yourself far too long. If you were my friend and I had cancer, you would beg me to get the help I needed to fight the cancer, knowing that if I didn't it eventually would kill me. I say the same thing to you. Sexual abuse affects almost all areas of our life, and if you don't get the help you need your pain will move into the emotional, spiritual, and relational areas of your life and affect you in a negative way.

From your question, you can see that it has already affected your relationship with your husband. Seek the help you need to deal with this trauma. I suggest a qualified counselor. Also talk with your spouse about this painful part of your life.

* *There is hope.* You are not alone. Hundreds of thousands of people have been sexually abused. (Today's statistics tell us about one in three young women and one in six young men will be sexually abused by age nineteen.) People who seek help do find hope and healing. The pain of the trauma doesn't magically go away, but with the right assistance you can live a very productive life and have an excellent relationship with your spouse.

* *God cares deeply for your pain.* When a person has experienced any kind of abuse, especially sexual abuse, it is very difficult to believe that God cares for you. After all, most likely you prayed for His help and you were still abused. There are no easy answers. We live in a sinful and fallen world.

However, over and over again in Scripture we see times of deep empathy from God. For example, the shortest verse in the entire Bible is "Jesus wept" (John 11:35). He wept at the death of a friend. If Jesus could weep over His friend's death, then He weeps for you in the midst of your pain and agony. The Bible is clear; God says, "Never will I leave you; never will I forsake you" (Hebrews 13:5). He didn't promise to take away all our problems and suffering, but He did promise to be there for us in the midst of our hurt.

4. *We are a blended family and my stepchildren hate me. My husband's ex-wife is negative and bitter about me and fuels the trouble I am having with my stepchildren. Any advice?*

You are not alone. Blending a family even in the best of situations is very difficult. You and your spouse will have to work very hard to keep the communication lines open as you fulfill your respective roles in the family. It's my opinion that your spouse has to take on more of the disciplinarian role because they are his birth children. He also needs to be the one to communicate what he expects from them in their relationship with you. His consistency will be very important. You are not their birth mother; don't even try to replace her.

And speaking of their mother, without knowing the circumstance surrounding the divorce and your remarriage, it is difficult to give much comment. However, for the sake of your marriage and the children, if there is any way you could communicate to her—either in person, by phone, or through a "nice" letter—that you do understand how difficult it is to be in her situation, then be willing to give it a try. Tell her that you will promise not to talk bad about her to the kids and that you will honor her as their mother. I doubt that she will become your new best friend, but she might lay off the attacks. Be above reproach in your interactions with her and others in the family. Even if she chooses never to take the high road, you must. The kids will eventually notice and respect you when they are older.

As for your stepchildren, find ways to be a cheerleader, encourager, and listener. Be good to them without any sense of expecting something in return. When they are at your home, cook their favorite meals and have a nice card and small gift for them when they enter the house. When something difficult happens in their lives, shower them with empathy. They didn't want the divorce of their mom and dad. Let them know you understand and care. You are in their life for the long haul, so start investing in them. It will no doubt take time and it might be messy, but healthy relationships win in the long run. Welcome to the blended family!

One last thought. Make sure the tension with the children and the ex-wife does not become the sole topic of conversation between you and your husband. I'm sure you are aware that statistics tell us that second marriages often don't last as long as first marriages. You don't have to be another negative statistic, but it will take your focus and resolve to make it work. It will require swallowing your pride on many occasions as well as serving the children *because of* your commitment to your husband.

5. *My wife is putting all her energy into raising our kids and very little energy into our relationship. Is this normal?*

Is it normal? Yes. Is it right? No! I am not suggesting that your wife abandon the children for you, but I do believe that you both have a responsibility to build into your marriage at the same time as caring for the kids. I mentioned this in chapter 1. The reason she may be putting so much emphasis on the kids is because she is not getting her emotional needs met by you. I have met very few women who do not respond positively to their husband when he sweeps them off their feet with acts of kindness and romance.

Perhaps before you had children, she was the initiator of time together and even romance. Well, now that there are children in the picture, you may need to make more of an effort to initiate romance between you. I find that the couples who do best with finding intimate times are the ones who work together to get the children in bed on time and who never tire of doing the special little acts of kindness toward each other. Your wife may not have her priorities right, but you can help her find those priorities again with an adjustment to the way you bring affection, warmth, and encouragement to your relationship. Before complaining about your spouse, be sure that you are doing all you can to fix the situation.

6. *I am drowning in work. My husband doesn't help much around the house, my kids are needy, and I am tired and irritable all the time. I don't like the person I am becoming. Help?*

As I mentioned in chapter 7, I was just on an airplane where the flight attendant said these very familiar words, "First put on your oxygen mask, and then help the person next to you." That's my advice to you. Your husband does need to help more around the house. Your kids should mellow out. However, since you find yourself in this place in life, first take a look inside and put on your own oxygen mask.

The term that many marriage experts use is *self-care*. Someone who makes self-care a priority is not a selfish person; she is a person who courageously finds room in her life to tend to her own needs *so that* she will have the energy to serve her family effectively. Didn't someone once say, "All work and no play makes Jane a dull person?" Tend the fire within your own soul and you will have enough left over to care for others.

Look for ways to replenish your soul. Build in times in your life where you are finding nourishment spiritually, physically, emotionally, and relationally. I know a mom of two preschoolers who finds most of the nourishment she needs by attending a mom's group at her church on a weekly basis and having her aunt baby-sit one afternoon a week. She has actually been known to just take a nap during that free time. She also arranges for a baby-sitter from her neighborhood to watch the kids for her weekly date night with her husband.

Speaking of your husband, he may be one of the people who are just dense about your workload; you may need to educate him about the situation. Sometimes it is as simple as asking for his help by giving him a "to-do" list that you both create. When you do ask for help, don't do it when you are irritable. Wait until a cool, calm moment. Don't say it in a judgmental way that will put him on the defensive; simply ask and share your expectation. You sound like you might already be in resentment and bitterness mode. If so, that is not going to help the situation or your workload.

7. We are drowning in debt. It is greatly affecting our relationship.

Debt and financial problems are one of the biggest blocks to an intimate marriage. A large percentage of divorces are caused each year because of poor financial stewardship. I don't have an easy answer for you, but I do have hope if you are willing to follow four financial decision recommendations.

A. Spend less than you make. You have to look at debt as slavery. Far too many couples live from paycheck to paycheck while going deeper in debt each month. Those marriages slowly die because of the pressure they live with concerning their debt. It would be wonderful to buy a new stereo, but if you can't afford to pay cash, *don't buy it.* I love cars just like the next person, but if your car payment is causing too much stress in your life and marriage, drive a cheaper vehicle until you can afford something else. Eventually every good marriage understands that the best things in life are not things! It is a proven fact that couples who spend less than they make are happier and freer to enjoy their relationship. Some of the most content couples I know are people who have very little financial resources, but they don't overspend so they are not under tension.

B. A budget is a must. When I was a pastor, I wouldn't marry a couple unless they showed me they had worked out a budget. Living by a budget is the single most successful way to spend less than you make and be a good financial steward of your money. A budget should not be created to be a burden, but rather to give you *freedom*. If you are drowning in debt and feeling the stress of finances, then you know that it takes a toll on relationships. The freedom a budget brings is the freedom not to have to focus on your money problems. Even millionaires, or should I say *especially* millionaires, live by a budget.

C. *Delayed gratification is the answer*. It takes discipline and self-control to delay a purchase. If you don't have the money, don't buy it! I am amazed at how many people live above their means and heap on the added pressures to their marriage and family relationships. We live in an instant-everything society, but the self-control to say no or to wait will not only bring you financial freedom, but a better marriage overall.

D. *Give 10 percent and save 10 percent of your income*. People who give at least 10 percent and save at least 10 percent will almost always have their financial act together. They understand stewardship, and this will translate into other areas of healthy living. If you don't currently have a savings and giving plan, then start small; but begin, even if you are in debt. The discipline will be good for you and the long-term health of your marriage. Someone once said, "There is no such thing as an independent financial decision." They were right. How you deal with your finances tells a story of the health of your marriage and family.

8. *My wife has a very poor self-image. No matter what I do it seems like she just can't overcome the negative way she looks at herself. Do you have any suggestions?*

I don't have any magic solutions, but it is very possible for your wife to reconstruct the way she looks at herself, and you can help her greatly with this very important task. A poor self-image often has its roots in childhood. You probably weren't around your spouse when she was growing up, but it is important to understand the tapes of her family system that might be playing in her head. For example, a person who was raised in a pessimistic home that withheld approval will often view herself in a much more negative and critical manner. Both spiritual and relational surgery will be required to reconstruct how your spouse looks at herself.

Help her understand that a low self-esteem is often caused by an improper view of God. The Bible actually says we were "created in God's image." The person with an improper self-image is often very hard on herself and unable to accept the grace and mercy of God. *God's part is:*

He created you.
He loves you.
He accepts you.
He forgives you.
He values you.
He gifted you.
You are His child.

Your spouse's part is to *accept* God's gift of grace. *Your job* is to surround your wife with *affirmation and encouragement.* Jesus believed in Simon Peter, and he became a great leader in the early church because of the faith Jesus showed in him. Helping your spouse develop a positive self-image is a worthy lifelong process. Help her find meaning and value in serving others. Help her be slowly transformed by the power of taking positive steps forward. Ultimately, her poor self-image can be changed when she continually taps into the grace of God.

My wife, Cathy, has struggled at times with an improper self-image. She is one of the most gifted people I have ever known, but she still struggles like so many people do with feelings of inadequacy. She finds a great deal of meaning in her teaching career with learning-disabled children. My job is to be her greatest cheerleader and encourager. I believe part of God's plan for Cathy's life is to be involved with those who are less fortunate. Just like Eric Liddell said in the movie *Chariots of Fire*, "I feel God's pleasure when I run," you can help your spouse feel God's acceptance as she finds her place of meaning and value.

9. *I love my spouse. I just can't stand the rest of her family, espe-cially her mom and stepdad. What is the best way to deal with in-laws who really are bugging me?*

Believe me, you are not alone on this issue! When you mar-ried your spouse, you also took on her family as part of the package. She is a product of her family of origin and you will never be able to wish it away. Here are my thoughts: Show honor to your in-laws, honor *on behalf of* your spouse. You show honor to people at your job, people who you don't nec-essarily like, and it seems to work. It is different with in-laws because you are more emotionally invested. I realize that one of the reasons in-laws can bug us is because we see part of our spouse's issues wrapped up in their relationship with their par-ents or siblings.

It isn't easy, but by showing honor to them you will be doing the right thing. You will have to decide how to show honor because every situation is different. It may mean not engaging in tense conversation at the holiday dinner table, because it really isn't the hill to do battle on. It may mean that you help support a sick parent for a season in order to honor your spouse. The best way to deal with a needy in-law is to support your spouse and pretty much keep your mouth shut.

The other "must" in dealing with your in-laws is to create healthy *boundaries*. This means that you don't have to engage every conflict. Be kind, but be strong about building the health of your own home. For example, if Grandma is a shame-based communicator and she expects you to bring the kids over for Christmas Eve and Christmas Day, you may have to tell her that you are creating your own Christmas traditions. You look for-ward to seeing her Christmas afternoon, but you have other plans for Christmas Eve and Christmas morning. Don't expect her to accept it without a bit of guilt being slung at you. Stay firm, stay strong, and stay the course while still honoring her.

If you and your spouse have a great deal of conflict over the in-law problem (and a majority of people do in at least one season of their marriage), then arrange for a "third eye." This means it is absolutely appropriate to get the opinion of another person. I would suggest a counselor or a pastor who can help mediate the conflict at hand. Problems with in-laws usually won't just go away. However, it is amazing what a little kindness, understanding, gentleness, and firm boundaries will do to help the relationship. Above all else, *honor your spouse*. In this situation it isn't about you.

10. *Our kids are getting in the way of my husband's and my relationship. I feel like my husband resents all the time and energy I focus on the kids. I am drained by the end of the day, and my husband doesn't understand where I am coming from. Is this normal?*

Yes, it is normal, and no, it doesn't always have to be this way. Your husband needs to get in the game and understand what a day in your life is like. He needs to show empathy and concern for the amount of energy you pour out on the kids, your work, and the home. Don't guilt him into trying to understand, but as often as possible share with him in a positive, non-confronting way about your life.

At the same time, as I mentioned in another part of this book, a child-focused marriage is not a healthy marriage. Your spouse does deserve more than your emotional scraps. I think you can rectify this pretty quickly by giving him TIME. This may seem like one more responsibility, but if you initiated one date night a week, a romantic experience on at least a weekly basis that he could look forward to, and one or two other times in the week when he knows you are there just for him, I think it will make a huge difference.

As time goes on, you both can share in the initiation of those experiences I just mentioned. I know this is going to sound like a slam to us men, but we really are quite simple. When you focus on your husband, it will actually enhance the relationship that you have with your kids. They will feel more secure when they see a loving marriage relationship, a relationship in which both parents give their time and attention.

Endnotes

Chapter One

1. Bill and Lynne Hybels, *Fit to Be Tied* (Grand Rapids, MI: Zondervan Publishing House, 1991), 23, 142.
2. Henry Cloud, *9 Things You Simply Must Do* (Brentwood, TN: Integrity Publishers, 2004), 43.

Chapter Two

1. Henry Cloud, *9 Things You Simply Must Do*, 103.

Chapter Three

1. Henry Cloud, *9 Things You Simply Must Do*, 72.

Chapter Four

1. Gary Chapman, *Covenant Marriage* (Nashville, TN: Broadman & Holman Publishers, 2003), 72.
2. Thanks to my good friend, Bill Hall, for this quote.
3. John M. Gottman, Ph.D., and Nan Silver, *The Seven*

Principles for Making Marriage Work (New York: Three Rivers Press, 1999), 26–44.

4. Ibid., 45.
5. Adapted from Willard Harley, Jr., *His Needs, Her Needs: Building an Affair-Proof Marriage* (Grand Rapids, MI: Fleming H. Revell Company, 1988).

Chapter Five

1. Les and Leslie Parrott, *I Love You More* (Grand Rapids, MI: Zondervan Publishing House, 2005), 123.
2. John Gottman and Nan Silver, *The Seven Principles for Making Marriage Work*, 149.
3. Adapted from Jim Burns, *The Youth Builder* (Eugene, OR: Harvest House Publishers, 1988), 219.

Chapter Six

1. John Gottman and Nan Silver, *The Seven Principles for Making Marriage Work*, 17.
2. Jim Burns, *The 10 Building Blocks to a Happy Family* (Ventura, CA: Regal Books, 2003).
3. As reported by Amanda Strindberg, "Exercising the Funny Bone," *Orange County Register* (November 12, 2005), 2. (Taken from a study by the University of Maryland Medical Center and reported in "Psychology Today" and "The Scientist.")
4. Doug Fields, *100 Fun and Fabulous Ways to Flirt With Your Spouse* (Eugene, OR: Harvest House Publishers, 2000) as listed in "Couple Minutes" from *Marriage Partnership* (Spring 2002), 8.
5. Louis McBurney, MD, and Melissa McBurney, "Touch Me—Not There," *Marriage Partnership* (Spring 2002), 28.

Chapter Seven

1. Corrie ten Boom and Jamie Buckingham, *Tramp for the Lord* (Fort Washington, PA: Christian Literature Crusade, 1974), 56–57.
2. Max Lucado, *In the Grip of Grace* (Dallas, TX: Word Publishing, 1996), 145, 148.

Chapter Eight

1. Gary Smalley, *The DNA of Relationships* (Wheaton, IL: Tyndale House Publishers, 2004), 47.
2. Ibid.
3. H. Jackson Brown, *The Complete Life's Little Instruction Book* (Nashville, TN: Rutledge Hill Press, 1997), 103.
4. Martin Seligman, Ph.D., *Learned Optimism: How to Change Your Mind and Life* (New York, NY: Pocket Books, 1990), n.p.

Chapter Nine

1. Paul Tournier, MD, *To Understand Each Other* (Geneva, Switzerland: Editions Labor et Fides, 1962).

JIM BURNS, PhD, founded the ministry HomeWord in 1985 with the goal of bringing help and hope to struggling families. As the host of the radio broadcast *HomeWord with Jim Burns*, heard daily in over eight hundred communities, Jim's passion is to build God-honoring families through communicating practical truths that will enable adults and young people alike to live out their Christian faith.

In addition to the radio program, Jim speaks to thousands of people around the world each year through seminars and conferences. He is also senior director of the HomeWord Center for Youth and Family at Azusa Pacific University, as well as an award-winning author, whose books include *The 10 Building Blocks for a Happy Family* and *Creating an Intimate Marriage*.

Jim and his wife, Cathy, have three grown daughters and live in Southern California.